Stories from the Rolodex

# STORIES
## *from the*
# ROLODEX

*Important Figures of Journalism*
*in Their Own Words*

## Beverly Stoddart

Composed in Whitman and American Typewriter ITC Pro at Hobblebush Design, Concord, NH (hobblebush.com)

Cover photo by Allegra Boverman (allegraboverman.com)

Front Cover Design by Renee Mallett (reneemallett.com)

Printed in the United States of America

ISBN: 978-1-73592-820-3

Library of Congress Control Number: 2020923411

Beverly Stoddart
Windham, NH
www.beverlystoddart.com

*For Michael*

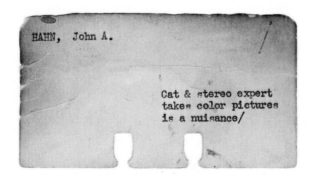

*Rolodex card from UPI's Boston Office*

"Follow the money. I have to do this my way. You tell me what you know, and I'll confirm. I'll keep you in the right direction if I can. That's all. Just follow the money."

—*Deep Throat played by Hal Holbrook in the 1976 film*
All the President's Men *directed by Alan J. Pakula*

# Contents

```
Boston Herald

Liberty 2-4000

Sam Bornstein
```

---

## Introduction

---

My journey to the Rolodex was an accident; a peek into the back room of
a shuttering business while working for a famous newspaper in a famous
city during a time when hustle and grit was how reporters made a name
for themselves. It all started in the last few minutes before midnight
of December 3, 1982, and the final countdown in a brutal fight. Media
tycoon Rupert Murdoch could save the Boston Herald from certain death.
Murdoch's News Corp wanted to buy the historic newspaper from the
Hearst Corporation, founded by William Randolph Hearst, famous for cul-
tivating yellow journalism. Hearst meant to close the paper due to loss of
circulation and revenue, leaving just one newspaper in the two-newspaper
town.

The opponents in the fight were five labor unions, including the
Teamsters, whose union was once considered the most corrupt in the
United States. The unions were required to concede to Murdoch's terms,
including a window in the contract allowing for non-union people to be
hired. Laid-off workers in seniority positions on the rehire list would be
abandoned for the term. Long-timers who should have been first up for
new jobs would be jumped over by younger hungry workers who would

never be allowed in a closed union shop. All terms had to be agreed upon for the sale to go through.

One man stood to speak to the crowded room of employees including journalists, salespeople, composers, and printers as the clock ticked closer to the midnight deadline - the president of the Newspaper Guild represented journalists and advertising. He spoke from the heart about "saving jobs, no, not all of them, but saving jobs was the right thing to do." The unions conceded, and Rupert Murdoch, who was known for putting bathing beauties on page three of his London tabloids, became the new owner. The difference between the stodgy standard-sized Boston Globe and the scrappy Boston Herald tabloid was apparent.

I was one of those who jumped the list and got a job in sales at the Herald. After working in Florida at the Fort Myers News-Press for ten years, my husband and I moved to New Hampshire in search of higher-paying jobs. Although, I got a sales job at the Nashua Telegraph in nearby New Hampshire, the Herald hiring window was big news. The thought of working at a newspaper in the huge Boston market excited me. I applied and got the job. Rupert Murdoch saved the Herald and got me one of the best jobs I would ever have in my newspaper career.

There is nothing like Boston. The people, the places, the history. It is special. The Herald had a luxury box at Fenway Park, and for all the Red Sox games I watched, it was from that fantastic venue. I saw the Celtics play from the Garden's luxury box. I attended lunches in the publisher's office, where we gave advertisers the special treatment. I participated in the turnaround and saving of the Herald from the brink of closure. I relished the fun fight of selling ads against the old-lady Boston Globe.

Driving into the Boston Herald from New Hampshire to One Herald Square could put you in a Martin Scorsese film imitating the iconic one-shot from *Goodfellas*. Instead of entering the Copacabana and passing mobsters at the bar, you come out of the highway tunnel and round the block-sized building to pull into an open-aired parking lot bordering the Combat Zone, Boston's adult entertainment area. You walk through the lot, stepping over used condoms left by prostitutes who plied their trade the night before. At the front door, you pass the security guard and head up the escalator. A left and a right take you down a long corridor passing the newsroom on the left, which stretches halfway down the hall. Howie Carr, a famed columnist for the Herald, shuffles down the hallway in a wrinkled Polo shirt, khakis, and flip flops. Next on the left is the morgue, where a staff of people clip stories and file them for the future. On the right is the accounting department with a credit manager who is more like the drill sergeant from *Full Metal Jacket*. He put fear in the heart of salespeople who didn't get cash with ad copy.

At the end of the hall, a left takes you into the advertising department opening to a vast room staffed with salespeople and managers. Jack Breed, the advertising manager, is in charge of the staff. He is as big as John Wayne and realistically formidable. "Ms. Stoddart," he would look down on me and sternly ask, "What have you done for us today?"

I can still see Jack staring down at me from his six-foot height. I wasn't afraid of him; I just respected the hell out of him. In his youth, he was a good baseball player and coached a team from the staff. His sales manager skill set included a coaching aura. The staff would meet every morning to apprise him of our sales success the day before, and you better had sold something, or he would not be happy.

Jack had this unbelievable comb-over hair that would fly away with a small breeze. He was always holding it in place or putting it back over from the left ear to reach the right ear. He was funny and thoughtful, demanding, and fair. Sadly, cancer beat him. I still think about him and get teary-eyed by his loss.

On the back wall of the advertising department were two glass doors leading into the office of the Boston bureau of United Press International. The glass doors were always closed, until one day.

United Press International was a news service and, at one point in its history, had more than 6,000 media subscribers. UPI covered the news stories around the world, with thousands of reporters filing news reports to newspapers, radio stations, and television stations.

UPI rented space at the Herald at a time when the news service fell into decline. At one point in its history, it sold for one dollar. Poor management and declining sales of its services made for the end of UPI.

A salesperson loves an open door, so I went in. Few people remained that morning. They were boxing up the remnants of the sad, dying news service. On one desk sat a dirty, steel gray Rolodex. I was drawn to it. It was probably the biggest one of its kind I had ever seen. The top was rolled away, revealing the cards attached to the wheel in the center. There were hundreds of cards. They were yellowed and had been touched and handled so many times, the edges were the color of toast beginning to burn. The cards were hand-typed, with many of them having cross-outs and hand-written notes added. Dates like 6/28/74 were added in the corner of the Newport, Rhode Island card, and phone number. Ask for Mr. O'Brien at the Customs and Immigration center at Logan Airport. The phone number shows as CA-3-2100. The Country Club could be reached at LO-6-0240. Mr. Jonathan Thomas of Winter Harbor, Maine's card was dated 3/17/67. Ask for Alan Friedberg at the Such Theatre. Talk to Joe McKenny of the Red Sox. His number was COP-7-2530. Boston Celtic's coach, Bill Russell's card, had his home address and home phone number with a note saying, "do not give this out." His wife's name is Rose, and his son is Jacob.

I saw history in the wheel of the Rolodex.

I asked the first man I came upon about what was going on with UPI. He told me they were closing shop, going out of business.

"What will happen to that," I asked, pointing to the Rolodex.

"Throw it away," he said.

"Can I have it?" I used the primary technique of any good salesperson; ask for the order. In this case, I wanted the old Rolodex. He gave it to me, and I carried it home to New Hampshire, where it sat in my closet for over twenty years.

I've been writing fiction off and on for years, hoping one day to publish some of my work. With each book, I struggled to get an agent who would help me reach my goal. I switched genres and tried my hand at horror fiction with two books about silk and invisibility. This was at a time before Amazon was invented and self-publishing was affordable.

And so, with yet another rejection in the mail, an agent wrote, "It's just too hard to get novels published today." She decided only to accept non-fiction works from then on. I ran to the closet and pulled out the Rolodex kept in a large, red suitcase and began going through the cards. One card, in particular, stood out. It read, "Baby Fiske, Liver Transplant." Who was the child? Did he or she live or die?

The Rolodex cards became more than hand-typed paper notes; they were lives. I realized it's not about getting published. It's about the people and their lives and how I can tell those stories. The strength of the words are what matters. Do they make you cry, laugh, care, and possibly change? The old saying is do what you love and you'll never work a day in your life. I found the love of writing by hearing the words of women and men who made their living reporting on peoples' lives.

*Stories from the Rolodex* is a "how did they get their stories" story. It weaves the tales of United Press International investigative reporters searching for the truth at a time when they had to find a telephone booth to call their stories into the bureau office. They learned how to tamper with phones in phone booths to make the calls if they didn't have coins in their pockets. Famed reporter and CBS news anchor, Walter Cronkite, was a UPI reporter and knew what to do on the street. Tom Foty tells the story of Cronkite being taught in Kansas City how to tap a telephone line without having to pay for the call. He learned how to use a pin to make a telephone connection. The "Most Trusted Man in America" who tearfully told us of President John F. Kennedy's death at one point in his career messed with payphones when he couldn't pay for the call but got the news reported.

UPI reporters banged on strangers' doors and asked to use the phone. The story needed to get out. This was investigative journalism at ground level. The reporters worked for the news service for very little money and loved what they did.

The big daddy of all books on investigative journalism is *All the President's Men* by Carl Bernstein and Bob Woodward. No one will know the source who is giving inside tips on a story that will eventually bring down the president of the United States. I remember reading the book and, of course, saw the movie with Robert Redford and Dustin Hoffman. They were journalists, and I had a Rolodex full of contacts used by a news reporting service. In January 2017, I began my journey to find people who knew, used, and were in that Rolodex.

In a Google search, I found a clip of CBS News National Security Correspondent, David Martin, who interviewed Bernstein and Woodward about the book when it celebrated the 40th-anniversary edition. A subheading was added to the cover, *The Greatest Reporting Story of All Time*. In an interview running on June 15, 2014, Martin says to the two men, "This is not a whodunit. Because we know whodunit. This is a howdunit. This is a reporter's procedural."

Bernstein agrees, "That's right. It is about reporting. It's all about the unglamorous how do you go about reporting a story. We went out at night and knocked on doors."

Woodward calls the Watergate reporting "the golden age of journalism." When asked if we are still in the golden age, both men reply, "No. No." Woodward adds, "The whole culture has changed. The internet age, everything is driven by impatience and speed, and what does that mean? We don't have that time to really dig into stories." Martin finishes with the thought, "The movie seems like an age gone by, except for one thing." Bernstein finishes the thought with, "Except for the way you do the work. If you're going to get the story, you still do it the same way."

I have always understood hard work. The first time I tried to sell an ad, I was 21 and came home in tears. It was just too scary to walk into a stranger's place of work and ask to talk to them about buying an ad. Luckily, my father-in-law was an old-timey type salesperson. He talked to me and gave me the courage to try again. Go fearlessly into the job. My mantra, in the beginning, was, well, they can't kill me. All they can do is say no. Then, I began to hear yes. You go out and knock on doors. You work the problem, find solutions. UPI had an army of reporters doing just that. But, all in anonymity. They received no notoriety or admiration for breaking important stories. They were hidden figures.

During Woodward and Bernstein's 'golden age of journalism,' United Press International journalists from all over the globe worked in this golden era. They filed stories on the wire to service-subscribing newspapers, television stations, and radio stations. They often didn't get a byline in the papers publishing their stories. Most worked for a barely living wage in which to support a family. These are the UPI reporters who are featured in *Stories from the Rolodex.*

Don Davis drove dark, dangerous back roads of the south during segregation. He had a gun in the glove compartment. Tom Foty covered one of the worst aviation crashes in history that occurred on Tenerife, one of the Canary Islands. The Boston bureau office covered airline crashes at Logan Airport. UPI reporters did this around the world before there were cell phones to help report the story. Jim Wieck helped to let the world know the Titanic had been found communicating through ship-to-shore radio. A skill he learned in Boston. David Tirrell-Wysocki, who worked for Associated Press, the competitor of UPI, witnessed the death of the schoolteacher, Christa McAuliffe, going into space. Unheralded reporters crossed the lines from safety to danger, all in the name of fair and impartial reporting.

Everyone knows Bob Woodward and Carl Bernstein of Watergate fame and the bringing down of President Nixon. Who you don't know are the equally talented journalists who worked the stories of a generation, and you read in your morning newspaper. *Stories from the Rolodex* puts a name and a face on the journalists who brought you headline stories. Every newspaper reader has read the news coming to us through wire services with credits like 'by United Press International' or 'by Associated Press.' Nameless, faceless writers.

*Stories from the Rolodex* explores how good journalism is investigated and written through anecdotes of important stories reported by United Press International journalists in the 1960s, 1970s, and 1980s. The interviews in the book are men and women telling true tales of what it's like to be on a battlefield with a pencil and paper, not a gun. Tom Foty takes you to the near-total destruction by an earthquake in Mexico City, where 10,000 people died and explains how they got the story out in a devastated country. When you read Richard Gross' thoughts of the "warmth of love at 77," you will hear his voice in the words. Karen Gray Houston will tell you what it was like being a young, black woman reporting on the story of Boston school desegregation. You are reminded of Paul Harvey's radio program, where we learn "The Rest of the Story." Only, this time, the rest of the story comes from the reporter who found it, lived it, and reported it in the UPI style of "get it fast and get it right." Andra Varin talks about the agony of working the third shift at the wire service. She tells the story of how the Boston Globe stole her lead. This was the fate of anonymous wire service reporters. Local newspaper editors could pick and choose what stories and what parts of the story they wanted to use from UPI. The source of the report was rarely named.

There were no cell phones. The internet had not been invented. The work had to be done on the ground by rooting out the facts and verifying them with qualified sources, so when they were reported, the story would be accurate.

The journalists who speak in *Stories from the Rolodex* passed through

New England in their UPI careers. Some learned their craft. Some honed their skills. All would fight the notion they produced fake news. The professionals who worked in New England and specifically the Boston Bureau of UPI followed the rules of journalistic ethics and ensured accurate reporting was presented to the newspaper, the television station, and radio station clients UPI served.

Why is the Boston bureau and the notes recorded in the Rolodex so important?

Read the news; a New Englander was there. The "shot heard round the world" was in Massachusetts. The world follows the medical reports coming out of New England universities. Boston-based FBI agents cracked the college admissions cheating scandal. Breaking news of national stories come from here. New Hampshire and the first in the nation primary is a mecca for political junkies. Doughnut holes were invented in Maine. Vermont gave us Bernie Sanders. Novelist Cormac McCarthy and actor James Woods are from Rhode Island. Hartford, Connecticut, gave us Mark Twain and "The Adventures of Tom Sawyer." And how can we ever forget, the 9/11 murderers came through Maine and then to Boston to attack New York. I can still remember standing in the Nashua Telegraph's newsroom watching the television with everyone and seeing the second tower crumble.

Walk down the hall of New Hampshire's largest newspaper, the Union Leader, and you will see the importance of New England in pictures hanging on the wall. William Loeb, the publisher of the UL, stands beside Aristotle Onassis. A campaigning George W. Bush shakes the hand of a young boy. You will see reporter Shawne Wickham's one-shot photo of the explosion of the Challenger shuttle. An original front page is framed of the reporting of the Japanese attack on Pearl Harbor. An oil painting of Daniel Webster hangs in the hall. The Union Leader quotes Webster on the cover of every edition. "There is nothing so powerful as truth," appears next to Old Glory on the UL masthead. What it doesn't have is the continuation of Webster's quote. He goes on to say, "and often nothing so strange."

Before there were computers, the internet, cell phones, and social media, we had to do things the old-fashioned way. We had to use typewriters with carbon paper if we wanted copies. We had to use a phone book or the yellow pages if we wanted to look up a phone number and then dial the phone. We had to write things down. And, if we wanted to keep track of our contacts, we used a Rolodex. Every office of United Press International had, at one time, a Rolodex full of the contacts an active wire service would need to reach a connection, a source. *Stories from the Rolodex* take the reader into the world of the working journalist at a time when reporters used rotary dial telephones. They looked up phone numbers in telephone books. Contacts were kept in a metal Rolodex sitting in an office where everyone could access names, home phone numbers and addresses, and clues about habits to land a story. The Boston Bureau's Rolodex is the junction for the stories in *Stories from the Rolodex*. The journalists and their words reveal the history and provide anecdotes to events that took place in the world. The interviews were done in person, over the phone, and in one instance, through an exchange of emails. Most were recorded.

You, too, have a link to these journalists who worked the busy wire service seven days a week, three shifts every day. It was grueling work with stories sent by wire, bells ringing on the teletypes, and rotary phones being dialed. The slot guy would take calls from reporters in the field and do the editing on the fly. Yet with all the chaos, there was craft taking place where the young reporters learned how to write a news story simply and quickly. It is time you knew who they are. There are seventeen interviews in the book presented in a question and answer format. You will hear their voices in their words and discover what real journalists have to say in *Stories from the Rolodex*.

UPI journalists got the job done. They went to the source of the story. They knocked on doors. They took hits from those who didn't want to talk. They did their job—nothing fictional here.

*Stories from the Rolodex* is a howdunit book where strippers and congressmen are chased and cornered and where politicians and reporters are stalked to save a life. Spin the wheel of the Rolodex and pick a card, any card. It will lead you to the Golden Dome for a drink or the No Name Restaurant for chowder. You could reach Red Auerbach at home. You can see where Henry Kissinger's ex-wife lived or discover Gloria's Cash and

Carry had luscious subs. You will see pictures taken by Wayne Phaneuf of Operation Homecoming when Vietnam POWs were returned to the United States in the middle of the winter, in the middle of the night.

The words, the voices, the thrill of the discovery of learning about these women and men who made up United Press International's anonymous army ferreting out facts will take you on the journey, and you too can learn about the genuine love of the work of reporting the news.

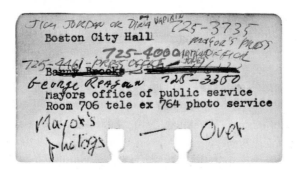

## *Chapter 1*

---

### George Regan—Rolodex Connection: Card on File.

---

*Press secretary to Boston mayor, Kevin White, Boston School
Desegregation, Rolling Stones Arrest, Big Handed Statue*

The first item to note on the Boston City Hall Rolodex card that shows George's Regan's name and phone number is that his name is misspelled and mistakenly written the way former president Ronald Reagan spelled his name. George and I met in the brick-lined conference room in Regan Communications' corporate office that is decorated with Boston artist Robert Kennedy's signed watercolors. Regan's a tall, handsome man, tan and well dressed in a blue suit.

He speaks with a Bostonian accent. Not the hokey "pahk the cah" kind of accent but earthy and local. He hunches forward and fiddles with a giant gold ring - the only piece of jewelry on his fingers. It's a Boston Celtic's championship ring. A real one. As he speaks, he slams the ring against the wooden desk, emphasizing every historical moment he has lived through, including the desegregation of Boston public schools. Regan spent a decade as a press secretary for Boston Mayor Kevin White from 1973 to 1984. He now runs the nation's sixth-largest public relations firm.

BS: *George Regan, you are the founder of one of Regan Communications, one of the largest public relations firms in the United States. As Boston Mayor Kevin White's press secretary, you faced riots, presidential candidates, and an angry Kevin White. First, can we talk about a relationship you had with the daughter of the head of United Press International? She was a Boston Herald reporter in the 1980s.*

GR: Anne's dad was Rod Beaton. He was the president of the entire worldwide operation of United Press International. I got a call from her one day that sounded kinda goofy. "I'm doing a story for the Herald on politicians," she says, "I've got ten summer reading books, and I want to know how many Kevin White has read." She reads the list to me, and I say, "Five." She says to me, "You must be working for a kind of stupid man."

"What are you talking about?" I ask.

She replies. "Ted Kennedy's read all ten." I said, "Are you out of your mind? Ted Kennedy just looks at pictures. He can't read." I was so mad. I know if this story runs on page one of the newspaper, Kevin White will have my head if he looks stupid compared to Ted Kennedy. I say to her, "I'm wrong; he's read nine."

"Too late," she says and hangs up.

So, I call the editor of the Herald and say, "Who is this idiot you have over there?" The editor friend, I know, replies, "She's very pretty." What does he do, he sends me her picture by messenger.

Fast forward, the story runs on Sunday. It's a killer. It kills Kevin White. I wind up seeing her, and we get engaged. And her father was the boss of UPI, and I didn't know that. I remember going down to her house at Christmas time, and I'd never been to Greenwich, Connecticut. The nicest family.

BS: *You were the youngest person with a byline in the Boston Globe. You were just 17. Can you tell me what you were writing?*

GR: I was a copy boy at seventeen years of age for the Boston Globe for an editor named John Burke, who was a suburban editor and Jack Thomas, who was the metro editor. For some reason, John Burke had taken a liking to me and put me on the one-to-ten shift or a four-to-eleven. Crazy hours. There was an issue with drugs being sold on Wollaston Beach in

Quincy. John knew I came from Quincy. The problem was jurisdiction. At that time, the forerunner to the state police was MDC, Metropolitan District Commission's police. They later merged. The jurisdiction problem was between the Quincy police and the MDC police. Nothing was getting done.

I spent about three or four months on it. Every day, the Globe would give me five dollars to buy a Coke and a hot dog and observe what was going on at the beach. I'd go back to the Globe, and I probably spelled cat, k-a-t, because I didn't know how to spell. I'd sit down with the rewrite guy and tell him what I saw. This went on for three or four months. Then the Globe published the story and ran it for seven or eight days in a row. That story really forced the authorities to make a lot of arrests.

The other story at seventeen I can think of was due to a guy named Jack Cullen, who was the midnight reporter. He got hit by a fire-hose cover. I don't know what the hell — some bizarre thing. I was a copy boy, and they asked me to ride along with the photographer all night. I always remember it was a July 3RD, and there was a flash fire that started around 1:00 am. I pulled up with the photographer whose name was Dan Sheehan. He was very smart. He knew that something happened there more than just a fire. It turned out the fire was set by one of the sons, and six or seven siblings died in the house. A horrible story. Anyways it was on page one, and I went back to the Globe that night sitting on the floor of the composing room watching my name go on the byline and going, "Wow." Pretty neat, but a big tragedy. And I remember going back to see my parents waking them up at 3:00 in the morning. I was very proud. I had a byline story.

BS: *How long were you at the Globe?*

GR: I started at the Boston Globe as a copy boy in 1970, and I stayed three or four years. I got fired by a guy named Matt Storin. He fired me on Thanksgiving evening because he was dating a woman named Madeleine Blais, who was married at the time, and he needed a position for her. I was kinda the young upstart, and he told me on Thanksgiving Eve, "Newspapers aren't for you." I was devastated, crushed. I remember I had to go home and tell my mother and father. It was awful.

BS: *He needed a position, and you had one, so you got fired on Thanksgiving Eve.*

GR: It worked out well. I remembered at the city hall, a friend of mine was an assistant press secretary and they were looking for tons of people. They said I was too young and immature, but a couple of people liked me. They asked for references, and I gave them some. They wound up calling Matt Storin. They couldn't understand why Matt Storin gave me such a horrible recommendation. I had a columnist friend at the Globe who knew me very well and said, "Matt is just Matt." This person picked up the phone and called Kevin White and told him the story. No thanks to Matt Storin.

BS: *You were going to be an assistant press secretary for Kevin White. I had read that he didn't want to hire you.*

GR: He didn't. I was hired as the assistant press secretary to Kevin White by Frank Tivnan. He was the director of communications. Bob Kiley was, at one point in his career, the deputy director of the CIA. He was a very serious guy. Kiley was then working for Kevin White. He loved government work. We had busing and all that. And my columnist friend, the guy that helped me, was the head of the spotlight team. He knew what's what, and he picked up the phone and called Kevin White and said, "I gotta tell you, this guy George, I know him well. He's gotten screwed by Matt Storin." And, that's what helped me. I didn't even know this was going on. It was well above my pay grade.

BS: *We're into your years with Kevin White. Mayor White was Boston Mayor from 1968 to 1984. You worked for him from 1973 to 1984. I read that White had a coalition of Italian, liberal, and black voters. How did an Irish guy pull those three groups together to vote for him?*

GR: It was '73 somewhere in there that I started working for Kevin White so I wasn't there in 1967 for that campaign. I understand it was a brutal, brutal campaign. He was running against a woman named Louise Day Hicks. She was very bigoted, very biased. Prior to 1968, the Boston Globe had never endorsed anyone for public office. They just had never done it. This, however, was different. She could not be mayor. She would have destroyed the city. They considered her a racist, a bigot, and destructive. She fed into bringing hate, and her audience was South Boston. I'm Irish. She was feeding right into the hatred. Kevin White had a movie star look. He was incredibly articulate. He had a vision for the city. Minorities liked him. Anyone with half a brain in the city liked him. Liberals liked him. It was a bruising contest, and he won for mayor.

BS: *Kevin White's slogan was, "When landlords raise the rent, Kevin White raises hell." versus Day Hick's slogan of, "You know where I stand."*

GR: Which means what? Hatred. It's as simple as that.

BS: *In the 1970s, Kevin White closed the "Little City Halls," and then he began copying Chicago's Mayor Richard Daley's political precinct machine.*

GR: What happened was Kevin White had a lot of intellectual thinkers around him, the Ira Jackson's, the Bob Kiley's, and Fred Salvucci. He was surrounded by smart people. He was running against Joe Timilty, who was totally unqualified, a wise guy. He associated with the wise guys. Not the brightest light bulb and Kevin nearly lost to him. I think Kevin had all these smart people around him who were doing great things. But at the end of the day, it really doesn't matter if they don't vote for him. So, he decided to do a blend of politics and a blend of the smarties. The politics have to get him elected, which is why he went to the precinct strategy like Chicago's Mayor Daley. Kevin and I went to Chicago, and Kevin introduced me to Daley not as his press secretary but as his son because I was so young looking. It's true. I sat in that meeting, and Kevin got it. You could not govern until you were elected. The rest of it is just hocus-pocus. He didn't change to the nuts and bolts machine politics. It's really difficult to blend both. If you have a ward boss, that ward boss becomes just as important as the police commissioner, the fire commissioner, or the chief of staff at the end of the day.

Kevin decides to blend politics with smarties, and he meets with Daley and becomes a machine politician. The problem with that is it can be near-fatal. Ward bosses mostly aren't college-educated. They don't have a moral background. They're big tough guys in East Boston. And I tell the ward boss, "You are as important as my chief of staff and my fire chief." They believe it. There are problems they create. You need somebody to monitor them. They're like wolves out there. No one's watching them. We're now focused on running good government, doing all kinds of wonderful programs.

Meanwhile, the banshees are out there doing whatever they're doing. They're shaking the people down. They think they're the big shots. They think, "I have permission from Kevin White." And that's some of the problems we had. The key is you got to watch them. That was not done, and that's what happened. All the foxes have raided the chicken coop. If you look at the history under Kevin White and urban America and you're trying to blend the two. It's an unnatural marriage.

BS: *On June 21, 1974, the desegregation of Boston Schools busing began. You were with the office at that time.*

GR: At the age of 23 years, I became the spokesperson for busing. My father's name is Senior, and I'm Junior. People thought he was the spokesperson. My father grew up in South Boston. He was very popular until desegregation and busing began. This goes back to the racial tension in the city. If you're Irish, they were saying how dare you to bring in these blacks and these Hispanics to South Boston? It was horrific.

I can remember that first day going up there being sick to my stomach. NBC News had more people in South Boston that opening day than at the Vietnam War protests that were going on at the same time.

BS: *The bigger story was busing. Not the Vietnam War protests.*

GR: Correct. I remember being at South Boston High, and I had a riot helmet on. It was just a disaster watching these crazy Irish people, my same country, my same heritage, screaming, "Fucking jungle bunnies go home." Are you kidding me? It was disgusting, and it went right downhill. It was ugly. They shot two police horses. They were giving horses apples with razor blades in them.

It was probably the ugliest chapter in the city. I had no idea what I was doing. I watched Kevin White, who did a great job. He went back and forth between the black community and the white community. A disastrous situation was created because of a federal court order written by Judge Wendell Garrity. He said later on, "I made a big mistake." Oh really?

The city is still paying the price for that today — totally inferior education. I mean, if you're an inner-city black kid in Mattapan, Dorchester, Roxbury, you're getting an inferior education. Meanwhile, we're spending about a billion and a half dollars for 53,000 kids, and out of that, only 33% are graduating from high school. Something's not right.

BS: *In 1972, Mick Jagger and Keith Richards of the Rolling Stones were arrested for assault in Rhode Island. It was two years before you started working for Kevin White.*

GR: I was kind of involved because I was working for the Boston Globe as a copy boy. And as I remember, Keith Richards was in Providence, Rhode Island, or nearby, and at the same time some disaster happened in Boston. (In July, 1972, there were three days of rioting in the south end of Boston known as the Puerto Rican riots.) I was too young to be over there, so they put me at the Boston Garden to take notes. The Rolling Stones concert was supposed to start at 7:30, and it's 9:30 at night. This is how Kevin White became a national star. He has a look. Every cop is dealing with this chaos. They had 200 cops at the Garden, and Kevin White gets a call that he has to do something. The Garden's going to explode. There's going to be a disaster. Kevin White calls, I forget who the Rhode Island governor is at that time, and explains the situation. White puts the Rolling Stones under his own personal recognizance. That's how he and the Stones became close friends. They send two state police helicopters down to Rhode Island to pick them up.

In the meantime, there's going to be a lapse of time to get them booked and up here. Kevin White is backstage, and I'm watching him. He's got movie-star looks. The kids are yelling and screaming at him. The last thing they want to see is a politician. They want the Rolling Stones. He tells them to "go fuck off" basically. "Pay attention," he says. He tells them what's going on. They got arrested. Big boos. Time out. "I'm in charge. They are in my custody. By the time they get here, it will be two hours. You can tear the place apart and not see the Stones, or you can be respectful. I got 200 cops here, but they're needed elsewhere. When I leave, they're coming with me." NBC was there. This is what made his career. He said, "What do you want to do?"

I was a little copy boy watching this, and Kevin White walks out with every cop behind him. They all left. Tom Brokaw was there. He does the story. Nothing happened at the Garden. They were perfect, and Kevin White became a rock star of his own. Fast forward, Kevin and Mick Jagger develop a good relationship for years.

BS: *Kevin White was responsible for the Faneuil Hall Marketplace revitalization in the '70s.*

GR: No Boston bank would do a loan. So, Kevin White had an idea. You don't loan money for that. Then you get no city business either. I'll bring my city business to Chicago. Kevin was tough. At the same time, he had a big fight with Jordan Marsh, the department store in Downtown Crossing, about toys. I remember being in his office. There was some charity, and they were being really cheap. Kevin has the CEO and the president come into his office. And once again, I'm there watching this all. He starts pulling out maps. This is like two weeks before Christmas, which is their busy time. But he says, "We have a big water main problem, and we're going to have to dig up the street right in front of the store." They got what they needed. Kevin White knew what hands to hold and arms to twist. I think I learned that fairly well.

BS: *You were the national advance person for Jimmy Carter and his run for the presidency in 1976. What memories of Carter do you have?*

GR: He was very sweet. I was brought on by Jody Powell, press secretary to Jimmy Carter. Kevin White was the co-chairman of the 1976 Democratic election committee with Jimmy Carter. Jimmy Carter was a one-term governor of Georgia, and Kevin was a big-city mayor. They both thought there was an opportunity for a different kind of president, and not just the Washington bred kind, a governor, or a mayor. I remember the New York Times wrote that Kevin White was going to be in the top ten Democratic prospects. Carter wasn't even on the list.

Long story short, busing comes along, and Kevin White's campaign is finished. The Globe does a big page-one story, "Kevin, won't you please come home." They had a map of the United States where they thought he'd been in the last fourteen days. That killed his campaign. Fast forward, Carter was running. I had met Jody Powell in Chicago, and going back and forth, we developed a relationship. Kevin was back in city hall dealing with a crisis, and Carter was on the campaign trail. Jimmy Carter was very sweet, just a sweet guy. They had all kinds of issues. Powell called me one day and wanted to know if I would get involved with the campaign. I needed permission from Kevin, which was not easy to get. I remember giving Jody Powell Kevin White's home phone number to call because he kept calling him in the office, and Kevin wouldn't return the call. On a Friday night, he trapped him. Kevin said, "If you want to go, then go."

I was afraid I wouldn't be invited back as Kevin's press secretary because Jimmy and Kevin were not friends. It didn't matter that they were both Democrats - a non-starter. Some of our people who had worked for Carter on a lower level got fired by Kevin. I was kind of nervous. I'm running around and checking in with Kevin, who was very cool. The day after the campaign, I was offered a job in Washington. Nothing high level, but I thought it was kind of neat. I remember my then-girlfriend was furious that I didn't take the job. She asked, "Why didn't you take it?" Cause I would rather be a small fish in a big pond than a minnow in the ocean. And Kevin never once discussed the campaign, welcome back and that was it.

BS: *You were an Eagle Scout. So was Thomas Kershaw, the owner of Cheers. I found it interesting that the two of you were incredibly successful, and you both were Eagle Scouts.*

GR: Jack Connors, the co-founder of the advertising agency Hill Holliday, was an Eagle Scout. I was an Eagle Scout. The head of Bank of America, State Street. There were a lot of them. I was amazed by the number myself. I got involved with the Boy Scouts when Regan Communications did some work with them. There is an amazing amount of people in this community who were Eagle Scouts and who play a role to try and make the communities better.

BS: *You read hard copies of papers. Why not the online version?*

GR: For me, I like to read the actual newspaper. I like to see the way the stories are placed. Okay? If the Globe is leading the paper on page one and that's a client, that's a bad day. If it's buried inside, chances are we can get away with it. There's not going to be much pick up. I like to feel and touch it. And I try to tell my young people here you don't see that online. You don't pick up. You miss it. I see that paper on my desk, and I'm looking for placement.

BS: *In 2018, you were number 71 of Boston's Most Influential People in Boston Magazine. You're on the list with the Governor, the Mayor, and Tom Brady. How do you feel about it?*

GR: My girlfriend said, "That's the best you can do?"

BS: *Can I ask about your ring? It's a Celtics championship ring. That is very cool. I mean, how many people have one of them?*

GR: The Celtics gave me a championship ring in 2008 when they won the championship. The ring has my last name and the number 17 engraved on it. It was the 17th banner, and it was also the seventeenth ring they made. Inside, it was numbered 1, 2, 3, 4, 5, so it happened to be the seventeenth ring made.

BS: *In the fourth month of Kevin White's first term, Dr. Martin Luther King was assassinated. You weren't there at that time, though.*

GR: No, but you know what happened, Regan Communications wound up representing Coretta Scott King, widow of Dr. Martin Luther King, Jr. in a legal battle for Dr. King's papers of which Boston University had possession. Dr. King had attended Boston University. I went to BU. Somehow John Silber, president of Boston University, got the King papers. Boxes of them and for BU, it was a big tax advantage. Dr. Silber was so busy. I think the King family assumed that the papers were being taken care of. They were literally in a basement being destroyed by water leaks. At the same time, they're building the King Library in Atlanta, Georgia.

We get involved with the law firm that is working for Mrs. King, and the mission is they want to go public finally. They are going the slow road through the legal process, and they want us to get the story out there about how these papers are being destroyed and falling apart. We were hired by Mrs. King which did not go over well with Kevin White because this becomes a huge national story. One day, I get a call from Kevin White, who was now working at BU. Whenever you get a call from Kevin White and he wants to take a walk is never a good day. We're walking along

Storrow Drive, and I know he's really mad because he's not screaming. He's just really upset. He said I put him in a really bad place. Dr. Silbur's president and I should have picked up the phone and told him what was going on. He said that Dr. Silbur is furious with me, and he even pulled the transcript of my records. He said they were less than impressive.

BS: *This is the stick he's going to use is that you didn't get a good grade in math?*

GR: That's what I'm dealing with. Long story forward, we won the battle, and Mrs. King has been in this office many times. That's how that went.

BS: *Do you have thoughts about Mike Dukakis, former Governor of Massachusetts, who ran for president?*

GR: I wasted a year of my life running around the country. I like Michael. I flew all over with him, and Kitty. I ran the Midwest for Dukakis and California.

BS: *Did you put the helmet on Mike Dukakis and have him photographed driving a tank?*

GR: That was the Midwest in Michigan, and I was blamed for that. But I was in California that day. And, I know exactly who did it.

BS: *1972 Kevin White was a possible running mate for George McGovern. But they went with Sargent Shriver.*

GR: Ted Kennedy put the boot to the nomination. Ted Kennedy did not want him. I got the book that McGovern wrote, and in there, McGovern wrote, "Kevin, I don't care what the hell Ted Kennedy said, you were the choice." And what happened was Ted Kennedy did not want to be superseded by Kevin White. They never really liked each other. Basically, Kennedy said to McGovern, pick Kevin White, we're not going to help you.

BS: *You had a role in the Kevin White statue that is at Boston's Faneuil Hall. It's ten feet tall. Why so tall? You spoke at his funeral. You were with him to the end. He had Alzheimer's.*

GR: I like big ones. I played a role in that. A little bit. A lot of people but I helped. Why 10 feet tall? He stood out. He was tall, and if you're going to put it in that location, it's gotta be powerful. You look at the statue; everything is big, the feet, the hands. Kevin was always in perpetual motion.

BS: *For all the years you were with Kevin White, how did those years affect you?*

GR: Probably for good and bad. I know myself I don't have the best of patience, and I got that from Kevin White. I'm not afraid to express myself, and that's not always the best thing I can do. And I can be tough. If you're going to be a leader, you cannot be a wallflower, okay? Take a position. We take a lot of positions in this company that are not good for business, but if God gives you a voice, then say it. That's good and bad.

*Chapter 2*

---

## Jim Wieck—Rolodex Connection:
## Boston Bureau Manager

---

*Riots, Fires, and Stonings; Finding the Titanic and Mexico City Earthquake*

When I first reached out to Jim Wieck, all I knew was he had been a Boston bureau United Press International manager. Among the duties of a bureau manager, besides wrangling a team of journalists who cover the news over three shifts, they work long hours for very little money. Bureau managers were expected to do every job. They write and edit news stories, manage the office admin staff, and answer to the many higher ups in the UPI news chain. They cover the work of others who have left work to go to the Golden Dome, the basement bar near the Boston statehouse. It is a thankless yet ultimately satisfying position. In one email exchange, he wrote about the Rolodex.

"It looks suspiciously like the Rolodex I used to bash in one of the phones on the division news desk in a fit of rage at New England Telephone and Telegraph. That would be the second company of that name and the long-lasting one, which became part of the current Verizon complex after the breakup of AT&T. Anyway, on some particular bad morning of phone communications as I was running the desk, I flew into a rage and grabbed the Rolodex and began banging it on the news desk phone. Cards flew out, and, after numerous bashes, the rotary dialing mechanism finally was shoved into the body of the phone for about an inch or so. Dave Haskell might recall the story, as I believe he was at the teletypesetter desk when I started the phone bashing exercise, and he jumped away in case stuff, other than the cards, started flying. Regardless, that old Rolodex got a lot of use, including the above re-purpose."

Jim and I finally got to talk when he returned to his home base of Dallas, Texas, from a 20-state, 30-day, 6,678-mile tour that included Louisiana, Tennessee, Michigan, Colorado, Oregon, and California. His voice is a mix of his home state Missouri accent, combined with a Texas drawl from his adopted home where he likes to "frequent Texas' many dance halls and honky-tonks for a night of live music."

BS: *Let's start here. What can you tell me about the Rolodex?*

JW: The Rolodex existed for decades before I got to Boston. It was big. The largest I ever worked with. We had them in almost every bureau. Boston had so many responsibilities for the New England states that they had to cover when other bureaus shut down. They had contact cards for people all over the region. Politicians, actors, sportspeople. I remember one of the events was when Jackie Robinson died. We grabbed the Rolodex and got in touch with his wife. She was on file, such things as that. It was probably the most important tool we used in the bureau. Of course, we also had phone directories from every town in New England. That was common practice in bureaus around the country. For example, in Kansas City, which was responsible for Kansas and Missouri, we had telephone directories for every city and town in both states. There were library shelves filled with telephone directories.

BS: *There are easily over 700 cards in the file, and I've barely touched them. Where was the office?*

JW: When I was in Boston, we were located in the Massachusetts Teachers Building on Ashburton Place. It's a little side street just off the capital. My period there was all at Ashburton Place. It was late August and early September 1972 when I went into the office. I knew absolutely nothing about New England politics and was told basically that I was going to be worthless to stay home until after the primary and then come in and help clean up. So that's what I did.

BS: *Where did you come from?*

JW: I had been a bureau manager in St. Louis, a much smaller bureau. We had four people on a regular basis, and we had a fifth on vacation relief. It was a key office that was responsible for covering the east side of

Missouri and southern Illinois. I was in St Louis from January 1970 to August 1972. I got there in New England in August of 1972 and left in 1976.

**BS:** *Why did they choose to send you from St. Louis to Boston?*

**JW:** Bill Ketter became the New England division manager, and I had worked for him. He was a sales executive in St. Louis, and so he pulled me to Boston behind him. He and I have stayed in touch.

**BS:** *I interviewed him. He's a good guy. Do you remember in 1973 that there was a Delta jet crash at Logan? What do you recall?*

**JW:** We got a call from someone who had been driving the perimeter road at Logan, saying there was a crash. I seem to recall that it was a photographer just roaming around looking for something to shoot and went to Logan because it was a foggy day. He or she might be able to get a shadowy image of a landing. But I'm not positive that it was a shooter or if it was a stringer or staffer. (A stringer is an independent contractor hired for a photo shoot or to cover a story.) At any rate, the person said they had seen a bright flash in the direction of the south end of the runway and was sure there had been a crash. We immediately pulled the airport cards from the Rolodex to call the tower, the fire department, and the cop shop there. Nobody knew anything. It took us a long time to confirm the crash. Twenty minutes seems to stick in my mind as we frantically kept calling those numbers, airlines, and other sources connected to the airport. Finally, we got confirmation and banged out a bulletin using, I believe, the airport fire department as the source. The crash occurred around 11 a.m., and I think New England News Editor Stan Berens, my direct boss, either was already down at the Golden Dome, the basement bar, and restaurant across from the statehouse for his liquid lunch or was just about to leave for it. At any rate, Bill Ketter, the regional executive, and Bernie Caughey, who both had been UPI staffers earlier in their careers, took over the writing chores.

After sending staffing to Logan, I began directing deskers and other staffers in making calls to sources, organizing what we knew, and didn't know, monitoring newscasts and radio news, etc. We all took dictation from our reporters as well as from stringers and other sources. But we did not do well against the AP. Mostly, I think, because we were too slow in banging out fresh leads. Bill and Bernie wanted perfect craftsmanship for each one. Sometimes you just need to fire off an ill-crafted one and start working on the next, hoping to make improvements each time. That's my take, upon reflection, on Delta 723.

The scene in the Dallas bureau was eerily similar when Delta 191 crashed on approach to DFW in 1985 in a severe storm and pouring rain. One of our Dallas staffers had just looked out a window and said DFW was really getting it when the call came in from a UPI technician attending a conference at a hotel just off the east side of the airport. He'd been idly looking out a window when he saw a huge flash and immediately called the bureau. "There's been a crash. I promise you. There's been a crash. I saw a huge fireball." But it was raining so hard he couldn't see anything after that. On that basis, I alerted photos and sent Dallas staffer Harihar Krishnan (yes, that's his name) with the first photographer, whom, I believe, was Gerald Schumann. I quickly followed up with sales executive Doug Page, who was the only other body available at the moment. Anyway, it was another scramble on the phones as nobody at the airport was aware of the crash. The downpour was just too heavy.

I think we finally got confirmation from the tower on that one. I don't recall who wrote the leads. It was one of our best writers in Dallas, possibly Mike Rabun, Southwest Division Sports Editor. I sat myself up as the funnel through which all information and notes came and parsed them out to the lead writer and those assigned sidebars. I pointed out stuff that I thought should make the next lead Graf and what should be up high in the story and other stuff that, while anecdotal, might be worth mention down in the body. Most of the anecdotal stuff I passed out to other writers for the sidebars and background stories. We did quite well in the 191 coverage.

BS: *In 1974, the US District Court ruled that the Boston public schools would be desegregated, and the Boston bureau dealt with covering the volatile situation. That was a big story.*

JW: Busing in 1974 was a big story. I remember the opening day of schools was filled with tension. We had a staffer at Southie, the South Boston school. During the course of that day, three incidents came up— all false, that just exerted enormous pressure on the bureau.

One was a report of a riot as the school let out, which was false. Another was a report of a woman being torched in Roxbury. Blacks had poured gasoline over her and set her on fire. The third report was that a gang of blacks had stoned a guy who was fishing on Dorchester Bay. They had stoned him to death. Those three things came up very quickly in order. The rumors originated in New York, and I have no idea the source of the rumors or how they came about. We ultimately knocked them all down and sorted it out.

I remember that much more than the school stuff because not much happened at the school. There were a few scuffles and kids taking a couple of swings. There was no riot. The torching incident turned out to be a mental case of a woman that the cops said had tried to do it before by pouring lighter fluid over herself. So that part was true, but she had done it herself in a suicide effort. The fishing guy simply had a heart attack and fell over, and the black kids were throwing rocks nearby. They were just walking home from school. There was tremendous pressure in those three cases to come up with a story that didn't exist. Most of our coverage was done by telephone back in those days, and the Rolodex came into play there because we grabbed the Rolodex for the Roxbury cop shop precinct. We got the word directly from the cops about the woman who was trying to self-immolate. Also, we called Dorchester and got the word on the fisherman directly from the cops, and our reporter at Southie knocked down the story of the rioting.

BS: *Dispelling these stories is part of the process of getting at the truth.*

JW: I remember I blew up at one of our New York managing editors. We were getting all these calls saying, "We're hearing these stories." Finally, I can't remember the guy's name. He was like the managing editor for the PM cycle, the afternoon newspapers. He called and said, "Your job is on the line." I just blew up and told him to go screw himself, and I didn't want to hear from him again. I figured that was the end of my career, but I never heard a word.

BS: *What were some of the big stories that the Boston bureau covered?*

JW: There were a couple of items that I thought were pretty important in 1975. One was the launch of the Bicentennial celebration for America.

That started in Boston, and we covered it heavily. I set up a separate bureau in Concord, Massachusetts, known for 'the shot heard round the world.' We had that, and it was a big event that required extensive planning and coverage. Gerald Ford had become president and had come to town.

The other important story was the release of the POWs from Vietnam and their return to American soil. Many of them came into Westover Air Force Base. I can't remember if it was decommissioned or was about to be. That was kind of a punitive deal by Nixon against Massachusetts for voting against him. At any rate, a guy named Wayne Phaneuf at Springfield, Massachusetts was the reporter covering that for us. He went to Westover, I think it was in Chicopee, Massachusetts and he did an outstanding job. He got a lot of interviews from those attending. Subsequently, he went on to go on to be the executive editor of the Springfield Republican and win a Yankee Quill award. Those were big stories.

And of course, any time a Kennedy farted, you had to cover it.

BS: *On your bio page on your website, www.wieck.com, two items are mentioned. First, the arrangement of ship-to-shore service for the discovery of the Titanic?*

JW: I learned that in Boston. Every now and then, a shipping vessel would get in trouble, and one of the things I learned about sea coverage was doing ship-to-shore, I think Berens taught me that. Stan was the one that said get on ship-to-shore, and that's where I learned it.

BS: *Does that mean you're on a radio and they are on the radio?*

JW: You're on the telephone, and they're on the radio that links you to the telephone lines. For the Titanic discovery, my bureau manager in Texas arranged for conversations every day. I think it was Frank Cook at the time. He got in touch with one of the financiers of the search for the sunken Titanic operation, which put us in touch with Robert Ballard. He was the guy that did the search. I set up the mechanism for the daily call. That was based on my experience in Boston. We had daily stories as they got close. When they first spotted the ship, UPI had the story.

BS: *That's a scoop. Second, was the reporting of a story of the deadly magnitude-8.1 earthquake that struck Mexico City in 1985.*

JW: My proudest moment. Everything went down in Mexico. There were absolutely no reports for the first 30 minutes or an hour. Everybody knew it was a bad quake, just not exactly how bad. I remembered that one of our photographers was an amateur ham radio operator. I sent him home, and he monitored ham traffic. I asked him when he could, to get participants in the discussion and get permission to use their quotes. When they got permission, he was to call us at the bureau with the quotes.

For the first hour or so after he got home, that was the only news we were getting out of Mexico. It was based on ham operators. Miami heard what we were doing, and they did the same with another staffer. That's how we crafted the initial stories for the first several hours.

Washington was getting information from the State Department, and eventually, they took it over. But initially, we filed it out of Dallas. My boss in Dallas was Travis Hughes, who became my partner when we launched Wieck (a communications and marketing technology firm). He called the Dallas Times Herald to see if they wanted to share a plane to get staffing into Mexico City. They agreed.

We picked a print reporter and a photographer. A woman on the staff who had radio experience went as well. That was our team. We sent them to Love Field. I told our folks to make sure we had a plane that we could radio communicate with the states. And I said, "If we don't, then don't get on that plane, only if we have communications." We got a plane and sent our crew down. I told our print reporter to go in and try to find the UPI bureau in Mexico City and if they had a story to go back to the airport to call it in. And he did.

But, when he got back to the airport, there was no plane. It had gone to refuel across the airport. There was another plane nearby, and he ran over to it, and it turned out to be, maybe Time or US News, somebody's plane, and nobody was there but the pilot. He asked the pilot if he could use their radio, and he said yeah. That's how we got that story out. That was thanks to Boston again. It was like ship-to-shore, it was plane-to-the-border as in the US border connecting back to a US telephone service.

BS: *I wanted to end with the Mark Twain quote that you use to sign off on your emails. "Do the right thing. It will gratify some people and astonish the rest." Why that quote? Is he a hero of yours?*

JW: He was and still is, and that's not because I come from Missouri. I go back to the wall telephone with the ring tone when you had to use three longs and a short and a third party on the party line, and when it rang, everybody picked up and listened in.

I think I read *Tom Sawyer* as a kid and maybe two other shorter stories, but I didn't read *Huck Finn* until I was an adult. When I read it as an adult, it had a profound effect on me. Huck after all the adventures down the river with Jim, he reaches the point that he ought to by law turn Jim in as a runaway slave. And in fact, he starts to do that. Well, he says, "I've got to do the right thing." And then it bothers him, and he finally decides. "My choices are to do the right thing or to go to hell." And he says something like, "All right then, I'll go to hell."

And I still remember when I first read it, that I damn near cried. That has stayed with me, and since then, I have read more of Twain's stuff. One of my favorites that I think should be translated into every language and handed out to every person who exists is *The War Prayer*. It's short, and you can find it online. But every time I see it in a bookstore, I pick it up and send it to a friend. Twain had a profound effect on me when I read *Huck Finn* for the first time.

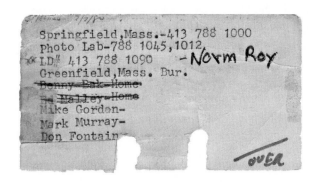

*Chapter 3*

---

## Wayne Phaneuf—Rolodex Connection: Stringer

---

———

"While at 'The Zoo' on January 24, 1973, I learned unofficially of the peace treaty from a Vietnamese repairman, and the news was greeted with both relief and skepticism. Eventually, on March 29, 1973, I was released. Stepping into the C-141 I had the biggest lump ever in my throat when I saw the American flag after what seemed like ages."

> *Henry C. Barrows Captain, United States Air Force; shot down*
> *December 19, 1972, released on March 29, 1973; buried at*
> *section 66 site 6758, Arlington National Cemetery*

———

*Operation Homecoming: American POWs Return from Vietnam*

In January 1973, Henry Kissinger, then diplomat for President Richard Nixon, negotiated a ceasefire with the North Vietnamese that ended the "U.S. military action" in Vietnam. The ceasefire negotiations included the release of all prisoners of war being held in Vietnam. There were 591 men brought home as a result of his work.

As a staff reporter for the Springfield Republican, Wayne Phaneuf did double duty working as a stringer for UPI. He has devoted his life to journalism and is currently in his 50th year at the newspaper, still working but now as the executive editor. In July 2018, Phaneuf was awarded New England Newspapers & Press Association's highest honor, the Yankee Quill Award. The Yankee Quill Award recognizes journalists with a lifetime achievement of distinguished reporting. Wayne Phaneuf spoke to me about cold winter nights back in 1973 when American POWs were returned from Vietnam prisons. Jim Wieck had called the coverage of Operation Homecoming one of the most important stories covered by United Press International in 1973.

BS: *Take me back to that day or days of Operation Homecoming.*

WF: It was so cold, and we were on the tarmac with all the reporters and photographers. My photographer, Ed Malley, got frostbite. He was working the camera, and back then, cameras were a little clunky. It stayed with him for the rest of his life. He didn't get anything cut off, but whenever it got cold, he could feel it in his fingers.

BS: *Were you and he both stringers for UPI working this event?*

WF: He was working the event for the Republican, but we did provide them with photos. He passed away at 43 or 44 years old about twenty-five years ago. I think about this event. It's so vivid, and it was pretty close to almost fifty years ago.

BS: *This is Operation Homecoming that Henry Kissinger negotiated for Nixon.*

WF: A lot of the men that came here were from here but a few of them from other areas. Westover Air Force Base is where they landed. It was a B-52 base. It's a monster size plane. I think, at the time, it was the biggest plane going. It was used to bomb Hanoi.

BS: *When they came home, who was there for them? Was it family only?*

WF: I think that was the case. Later on, when there was Desert Storm, they would come back to gigantic welcome home events. But at that time, I think it was family only and the media. The other thing was it was in the middle of the night. They came in from other bases and had to refuel. For some reason or another, I can't remember any of them being in the daytime.

BS: *It was the dead of the winter of 1973.*

WF: It could have had to do with the anti-war movement too.

BS: *That was still present then?*

WF: There was still a lot of the war in 1972 and 1973. As a matter of fact, at the gates of Westover, there was at least a weekly group that protested the war. A little bit different today.

BS: *You see this giant plane landing.*

WF: They were keeping us apprised of when it was coming. I have to tell you it's hard for me even to talk about it. It was pretty rough stuff. Some of these kids hadn't seen their fathers in five or six years. It was quite a moment of pure joy. Unfortunately, I think several of those marriages didn't last just because of what had happened to these guys.

BS: *What condition were these guys in when they got off the plane?*

WF: They were all mobile. They weren't going to take people back that were bedridden.

BS: *Did you get to talk to them?*

WF: We didn't get availability to talk to them one-on-one, but several of them walked up to a microphone and spoke. There were kids running across the tarmac. It was even worse for me because my brother was still in Vietnam at the time.

BS: *Was he still an active-duty soldier?*

WF: Oh, yea.

*Photos courtesy Wayne Phaneuf. Left: A soldier speaks to the reporters covering the event. Right: Children, who have not seen their fathers in some instances for years, run to greet their loved ones.*

"Arthur was released with 141 other prisoners on February 12, 1973. One month earlier, he had been offered an earlier release, but he replied: "No. I'll go home in the order of shoot down. We had all agreed that the sick and wounded would go first and then by order of shoot down."

Arthur was in the second group to load onto an airplane, and he reunited with his family at Westover Air Force Base at 20° below zero weather. He had not seen his wife for seven years, and his four children scarcely knew him. Arthur recounted the reunion: "It was a pretty traumatic experience getting released. A lot of ups and downs. On the third day, my wife wanted a divorce. I should have given it to her, but I tried to make it work." They divorced in 1977."

*Arthur Cormier, Air Force from 1954 to 1984. Retired as a Captain. Held prisoner for seven years, three months, and one day. Lovell Historical Society, Lovell, Maine*

———

**BS:** *They had been there so long they didn't think it was possible?*

**WF:** For some of them, it was a long, long time. And a lot of them weren't sure they were ever going to come back. There wasn't a list of who was there. Some people just disappeared and weren't on the list as prisoners.

**BS:** *Isn't that the POW-MIA movement?*

**WF:** Even some of them were found. It wasn't like the day after Hanoi called and said we've got these guys in prison. The only reason Hanoi mentioned they had prisoners was to ramp up the idea that the war should end a little bit sooner. One of the guys from here was named Sullivan. And he went back to the Air Force and was there for quite a while. He stayed enlisted.

**BS:** *Wow. Wouldn't you want to get out?*

**WF:** Yes, but for some, the military life is really hard to walk away from, especially pilots. It was interesting the contrast of what happened in Desert Storm and Operation Homecoming. They had a brass band and hundreds of people waiting for people to come home just twenty years later.

**BS:** *As a result of this reporting plus your life's body of work, you won the Yankee Quill Award.*

**WF:** I've been here for fifty years. It's a lot to go through. Consider the Watergate years and that brief period when reporters were revered. Not so much today.

**BS:** *In your fifty years at the Republican, what stories stand out to you?*

**WF:** I covered riots in Springfield with school busing and covered that story for a number of years. That finally got settled. All the predominantly black neighborhood schools were falling down, and the white neighborhoods had new schools. I happened to grow up in one of the predominantly black neighborhoods. I got involved in that early on. We really did a lot to try and make things better. I covered it for about eight years, and it took twelve years for it to become law where they couldn't have ninety percent in one school and ten percent in another.

BS: *What were some of the saddest stories that you covered?*

WF: There were so many of them. I remember a lot of these stories were before there were cell phones. You go out, and you're not sure what you're getting into. I had one that I remember that I can close my eyes and see it. There was a pickup truck that turned over on the turnpike. They were going down a long, long hill in the Berkshires. I was told there was a bad accident. It was a family of five, and the pickup truck caught on fire. They all were killed. The horrible thing about it, they were driving and behind them were the grandparents in their car. That just added to the horror of it all. The accident happened in the middle of nowhere, and I had to get the story out. I hopped a fence and walked to a house about a mile away. I knocked on the door and was lucky that I didn't get shot and asked if I could use the phone and called the story in.

BS: *You told them you were a reporter, and you needed a phone.*

WF: Yea. At the time, I wasn't exactly clean-shaven. But they were country people, and they let me in. I had really long hair and a beard. I used to write a column called Vibes. I started in 1969.

I worked for the Springfield Daily News, the afternoon paper. I would be on the road for two weeks and not come to the office because it was all done by phone. You get to the point where you could pretty much have your lead and sentences all set. You don't get much of that anymore. We got the job done in a good way.

———

"Four months after Alan Brudno's homecoming, his in-laws found his body, fatal traces of phenobarbital in his stilled veins. He was the first of the 566 returned Vietnam POWs to die. It was national news." "Brudno spent 7 1/2 years in Vietnamese POW camps...he became the first veteran who committed suicide after returning home to have his name engraved on The Wall."

*"Eleven Letters Honor POW's Hidden Wound" by Monte Reel,*
*May 22, 2004, The Washington Post*

———

*Chapter 4*

---

## Karen Gray Houston—Rolodex Connection: Boston Bureau Reporter

---

*A Black Woman Reporter in the Time of Busing in Boston*
Talking with Karen Houston was like talking to an old friend. We had never met, but it was relaxed, friendly, and with laughter. She is the niece of a champion of the Civil Rights movement, Fred D. Gray, whose accomplishments include representing Martin Luther King Jr. and Rosa Parks during the 1955 bus boycott. Her father, Thomas Gray, was a boycott leader and eventually became a federal judge in Alabama.

Karen's new book is a coming-of-age memoir titled, *Daughter of the Boycott: Carrying On a Montgomery Family's Civil Rights Legacy.* It is published by Chicago Review Press, and is available now.

Here is a transcript of our conversation. We start by talking about the Rolodex.

BS: *Do you remember the Rolodex?*

KGH: First of all, I can't believe somebody found the Rolodex. Second of all, we were going to throw it away?

BS: *Crazy huh? Let's jump right in if that's okay with you?*

KGH: That's okay with me. I feel like I'm going to be a teeny tiny part of whatever you are writing because you're writing important stories that jumped out at you from the Rolodex. You want to put it into context by people who worked in the bureau.

BS: *We start with you at UPI in Boston.*

KGH: That was in 1973 after I had graduated from Columbia's Journalism School. I went to Ohio University and got a degree in psychology and did some work on campus writing for the newspaper and radio station. I said that seems like fun, let's go to journalism school. Fred Friendly was my adviser. He used to be president of CBS News and worked with Edward R. Murrow. He encouraged me to go into broadcasting though my initial interest was in print. I thought I wanted to be a newspaper reporter. However, I couldn't find a job right away. First of all, my father pulled the plug on the cash and said, "You've got to come home. You can't wander around New York looking for work." So, I sent out a gazillion resumes and tapes looking for a radio and TV job which didn't develop right away. I received an unsolicited letter from UPI.

BS: *First, would you say your father's name for me?*

KGH: Thomas Gray.

BS: *He said, come home. We're not spending any more money.*

KGH: Well, they paid my way through undergrad and graduate school, and truth be told, dad wanted me to go to law school. I didn't want to do that, and he said come home. He knew a lot of people in Cleveland. He could help me find a job in Cleveland. I didn't want to find a job in Cleveland.

I got that letter from UPI a few months after I had graduated saying, whoever wrote it, I can't tell you the name of the person, "What are your journalistic goals, now that you've got your master's degree? We may have an opening for a reporting job." I called them. They said to come to New York for a writing test, and I did, and they told me they had an opening in Boston. So, I went. My parents were not excited about the prospect. My father said, "Well, you know Boston is a long way to go and a really big city for a young girl like you to live by herself."

BS: *But you were in New York?*

KGH: I was living in a dorm, going to graduate school. I'm just saying.

BS: *That's a dad talking.*

KGH: He was not going to support me financially doing that. He gave me about $200. One of my best friends had just graduated from law school and had a new car which we wanted to put on the road, so she drove me up. I lived at the Y in Cambridge. It was the best I could do. It was a room with a bathroom down the hall, and I stayed there until I made enough money from UPI to rent an apartment in a house in Cambridge.

That was that. There was pressure on media establishments to hire minorities. People would go to Columbia looking for graduates, period. I'm sure people were looking for black people. You know newspapers and etcetera would go there and say do you have any suggestions for your recent graduates.

BS: *Right, but you had a masters. You'd gone above and beyond.*

KGH: Right, but I was still black. Anyway, I figured it was one of my professors, either Fred Friendly or Norman Isaacs, my newspaper professor. He liked me and tried to get me a job with the Detroit Free Press when an editor had come to town. But I had decided in my head. I was not going to live in Detroit or Cleveland. I didn't pursue that. I'm assuming that somebody at Columbia referred me to them or them to me. I never found out.

BS: *And what assignment did they put you on when you got there?*

KGH: The overnight. Midnight to eight. And basically, the only thing I was doing was rewriting articles in the newspaper for the radio wire.

BS: *Okay.*

KGH: I would do that. Here is something kind of interesting. I think if I can recall this correctly, there was a union rule about how long you could keep someone on an undesirable shift.

BS: *I think you're right.*

KGH: They would keep you on that midnight to eight for six weeks or a couple of months or something. But they had to put you on a day schedule for a while. And, they didn't do it for a long time, but they'd put you on a day shift, and that was when I had an opportunity actually to go out and do some field reporting.

BS: *Do you remember any of the stories that you reported on?*

KGH: Yes. We didn't have a huge office. It was a small bureau with a handful of fairly young reporters and editors and writers. We were mostly fresh out of college. There were a couple of older guys more veteran than we were, maybe in their thirties that were doing political news at the statehouse. The rest of us were out in the field at the time. In the 1980s, the busing story was the big story in town. I remember that it was a terrible period to be covering the news and to be a black person in Boston. I was shocked twenty years after Brown v. Board of Education and the Montgomery Bus Boycott to be in a northern city that called itself 'the cradle of liberty' and to see that level of racial hatred and violent protest directed at black people.

BS: *Did you cover the first day?*

KGH: I don't believe I was there that first day, but I did cover many of the other days. I remember covering the day when the National Guard got called in. I didn't see the first day when the white kids and some of their parents were throwing rocks at the kids at Roxbury at the school bus when they arrived. I wasn't there that day, but I saw similar things on other days. I remember the climate at the time. You had to get to stories sometimes in taxis. I remember one time, a taxi driver refused to take me into South Boston because so many bad things had been happening. There was so much violence directed at black people that he thought he was doing me a favor. I ended up having to get in a cab with some white reporters so I could do my job.

BS: *So, he would have taken you anywhere else but there.*

KGH: Yea.

BS: *Tough times. Did you ever get hurt or attacked in any way?*

KGH: I was never hurt; no. Might have been called some names or something or you got the look. I never felt comfortable in Boston. I didn't even like going downtown to shop in Boston. I used to think, wait a minute, where are all the black people? Black people stayed in their little neighborhoods, Roxbury and Jamaica Plain, and you didn't feel right. And you went into the stores, and it's similar now, you go in, and you get followed around because everybody thinks you're going to try and steal something. I get that now.

**BS:** *But you did your job. Do you recall other stories that you covered? What did they make you do? Did they give you any good assignments?*

**KGH:** I got some great assignments. Wilbur Mills came into Boston chasing after Fanne Foxe. I don't know if you remember that story. The congressman, who chaired the House Ways and Means Committee, and was having an affair with a stripper. They called her the Argentine Firecracker, Fanne Foxe. She had come up to Boston to perform, and it happened at a strip club on a Saturday when I was the only reporter available in the bureau.

I had never been to a strip club before. But I went, and there were a handful of reporters, and we went inside. This club was sort of a theater. It wasn't like a bar. It was a theater with a stage and was pretty sleazy. These women would come out and bring a towel, throw it on the floor and roll around and take their clothes off. It was just really pretty disgusting. We sat there because we were hoping to see Wilbur Mills. After a couple of the performers had performed, she was about to come on. Wilbur Mills came in and sat in the middle of one of the rows and watched her perform it. When she finished, he finished, and he got up, and we followed him downstairs to her dressing room.

**BS:** *The guy in politics doesn't even care if reporters are following him.*

**KGH:** Here's what we all found out. Mills was an alcoholic. He had a serious drinking problem, and there had been some episodes in Washington and all that. But, when we went downstairs, there was this thin wooden door with a gold star painted on it because she was the star performer. We just waited because there was one way in and one way out. He had to come out eventually. So, I guess they said he might as well go out and give them a statement. He came out with her and stood beside her and told us that she was a family friend, a friend of his and his wife. She was a family friend, and he was coming to watch and support her performance.

**BS:** *Well, how nice was that?*

**KGH:** I halfway remember writing the story about it and saying something like, "She may have been the stripper from the Silver Slipper, but she had her ways and means." It was probably one of my most fun UPI stories ever.

BS: *Great line. That's a great story. How old were you at that time?*

KGH: I must have been twenty-three. Oh my god, it was incredible. It was my best time. I think it was an odd time to be in Boston, and I have one more thing for you for Boston, and it is sort of related to the Rolodex. I had to learn the Rolodex, for one thing. I was coming out of graduate school, and it's not as if we students had a whole Rolodex full of files of important people. So, I had to learn what it was, and they treated it like this is an important thing if you need someone. Especially since we were often working there on weekends and nights at times when you didn't have access to people, you could go in there and look for somebody and call them on the phone.

One Sunday, I was working at the bureau. I was probably the only person in the bureau other than one or two teletype operators and a photographer. And what happened? There was news that broke, and it was about Father Robert Drinan. He was a congressman. He was a Jesuit priest, and I think he had gone to Georgetown, but he was in congress. Eventually, he gave up his career because the pope at the time said that priests who were involved in politics had to make a choice. Pick one. At that time, it was during Watergate and either the news, and my mind is fuzzy about this, either he had been named to Nixon's enemies list, or he became the first person to call for Nixon's impeachment but not over Watergate over the secret bombing campaign over Cambodia. Whichever, they were both good stories. But it was up to me to try to catch up with him somehow. Somebody thought that he might be in Boston and not in Washington, DC. He might have come home for the weekend. So, pull out the trusty Rolodex.

I'm sure they have updated the files since then because this was like 1974 or something like that. I looked for a number for Drinan, but I think that the numbers we had at the time were for his Washington office and his Boston office. I don't know if there was a home number or if there was a home number, I might have called and didn't get an answer. Sometimes the numbers didn't get updated.

So, what happened was, I was going, "Oh my god." I'm sure some editor who was in charge that weekend was calling me up going, "We got to get him because we heard he's in town." And I'm going, "How? I can't leave the bureau. How can I find him?" I hung up the phone, and I dialed the operator. I *dialed* the operator. It was a time that was even before 411, right?

BS: *The phone is a rotary dial telephone.*

KGH: 'O' for the operator, zero. The operator gets on the phone, and I introduce myself and tell her I'm working for UPI, I'm Karen Gray. We're trying to reach Father Drinan for a story. I'm sure I explained what the story was. Do you have a number for him? And she said, "Oh wait a minute. It's Sunday afternoon. He's probably over at his brother's house because they always go over there after mass on Sundays for dinner."

BS: *Oh my gosh. Really?*

KGH: I swear to God. She gives me the number, and I call the number, and he is over there, and he talks to me on the phone. I get him.

BS: *You went from UPI to WHDH, right?*

KGH: They were two great places to work in Boston. Here's how that happened. You know Fred Friendly, friendly Fred, had been encouraging me to get into broadcasting. He thought I had some talent, and he had suggested that I talk to a friend of his who was the news director at the NBC affiliate or owned the station in Cleveland where I grew up. He gave me an interview at the time but said, "Hey kid, go get some experience and come back." I was sending out lots of resumes and tapes, radio tapes and TV tapes all over the country. I had a copy of Broadcasting Yearbook that listed every radio and TV station in America. I was sending out tapes to places I thought I wanted to live in or wouldn't mind working there. I had just inundated the Boston market. I was acquiring a stack of rejection letters that were about a foot tall.

BS: *You were doing this all before cell phones, the easy way we have of communicating today, right?*

KGH: Yes, it was in the olden days, Beverly.

BS: *I know, I know. I'm old enough to know.*

KGH: I wrote this one letter and sent a resume to WHDH and got back another rejection letter. Sorry, we don't have any openings right now. We'll keep your resume on file — yea, yea, yea. I was sending out all this stuff while I was working at UPI, but I was going to get a better job.

BS: *Did you feel UPI was going down the drain? Or was it too early for that?*

KGH: There was some sense of it, but I didn't think that I would be around for it.

BS: *And you wanted to be in broadcast?*

KGH: Exactly. For a second, I thought of UPI Audio and UPI Radio, but I wanted to be at a station so a year after I got that "we'll keep your letter on file," I got a phone call from Nick Mills, who was the news director at HDH. And he said, "Hey kid, you still looking for work?" And I said, "Yes." He hired me as a reporter/anchor. I anchored on the weekends, and I reported three days during the week.

BS: *That's awesome. You go from UPI print straight into radio, but you also worked for ABC, CBS, and NBC?*

KGH: WCBS TV, in New York, the local CBS news station. And for NBC, I covered for the Reagan White House.

BS: *Did you work for Jim Wieck in Boston?*

KGH: I did. Jim was like a little newshound. He was just so serious about the news, and I liked working with him. I got to feel that he enjoyed being the bureau chief. He liked that job. He felt pride for the people who worked for him. He was living and breathing UPI.

BS: *I've been trying to find women to talk to about that time and the Rolodex.*

KGH: Call Janet Wu.

BS: *That's Janet Wu from WCVB. I will try to reach her. I'll see if I can get her on the second one.*

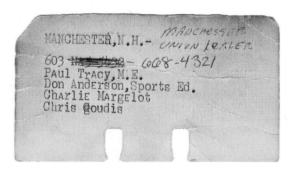

## Chapter 5

### Joe McQuaid—Rolodex Connection:
### Former Publisher of Union Leader, Card on File

*Jimmy Hoffa, Loeb Letters to the Editor, Live Free or Die*

Joe McQuaid is fearless. When Joe and I initially spoke, he was publisher of the Union Leader. Since then, he has turned the leadership post over to his son, Brendan. Joe is still listed on the masthead as Editor-at-Large. The Union Leader is New Hampshire's only statewide newspaper. As publisher, Joe would talk to anybody: presidents and hopefuls and subscribers who want their newspaper on the porch and not in a bush. President Donald Trump called Joe, "a real low-life."

Joe stands on the shoulders of newspaper giants: William Loeb, with his outrageous page one editorials and Edmund Muskie's tears and Nackey Loeb, William's wife, who took over the post of publisher at the Union Leader when William died. Joe is a great storyteller. No wonder. He has the stories to tell. He can speak on any subject, find humor in it, and educate with minutiae bits about it. In 2017, he published a book about the Cog Railway, the famous mountain climbing locomotive of Mount Washington, the highest peak in the Northeastern United States. The book was censored by the Cog Railway gift shop due to the subject of the tragic turn of events. We met in his office at the Union Leader, and of course, he started with his humor.

BS: *Do you mind if I record our meeting?*

JMcQ: It's like the white house. The recording is voice-activated (he said jokingly referring to his office). It goes on automatically. The recording was before Nixon, who had it on everything. Guys like Kennedy would do it on certain things. Roosevelt had it back in the day.

BS: *I wanted to start with UPI and your random thoughts and feelings. Didn't you have both services here?*

JMcQ: We had both services when I was first here as the office boy at age 15. Among one of my many jobs was cutting the wires from the teletype machines. We had a whole room devoted to wire service machines - machines from Associated Press and UPI and a couple from Race Wire, as in horse racing. And then for a while, I covered the Manchester Yankees baseball team wire. We shared among the papers that had AA baseball teams. The main ones were AP and UPI, and I had to cut those wires on Saturday nights as the office boy for the benefit of the wire editor.

BS: *When you say, 'cut the wire,' this is a continuous roll of paper?*

JMcQ: I had to cut the roll of paper. Depending on who the wire editor was, I had to cut the individual stories to place on the person's desk or give the roll to the wire editor who would go through them. And you had to make sure you had the numbers not obliterated. The numbers were on the top of each story, and they corresponded to the teletype. I can't remember the technical term for it, but it was a little strip of paper that got fed into a machine that turned that into type so that our guys in the composing room did not have to knock out all these wire stores in addition to all the reporter's stories. That was a real godsend technological advance. Before I came to the paper, I had to make sure those numbers were on there. A wire editor would circle the numbers of the stories that he would want to use, and he would put those in a box, a wooden box, and send it upstairs in something like a little elevator. (Joe refers to a picture in his office of the old office that had a wooden box on the desk.) That's Amherst Street, and the picture on the right is the newsroom guys in the forefront are at the copy desk, and two of them are sitting on either side of a wooden box on a brass pole. You would press that, and the box would go up to the composing room and, the guys would look at the numbers on the tape and set them in. That was my first experience with the wires. And then when I was, fast forward, to be the Sunday editor, I would go in and look at the wires myself periodically on Saturday. I wanted to check what stories I was going to use on the front page of the first section, versus the wire page. We had one page just for wires for the Sunday News. We were mostly local, but if it were a big story, it would be on the front page of the A section.

BS: *When you used the wire stores, did you use them verbatim? I understood the names of the reporter would be taken off.*

JMcQ: If it were a wire story and had a name on it, I would probably use the byline of the wire service reporter. There were famous national bylines of UPI writers, Quigg. I remember one whose name was Doc Quigg. It was HD, but he didn't use Doc in the byline. His friends called him that. I met him in New York at a reunion of World War II correspondents.

BS: *Because of your father?*

JMcQ: My father had passed away, and Doc Quigg had come up here to cover a very famous murder trial of a doctor, a real doctor from Candia, New Hampshire. His name was Herman Sander and was accused of a mercy killing. The year was 1950. Sander was accused of administering an air embolism to a lady who was dying of a very painful form of cancer. There was a jury, and the state prosecuted, and this went everywhere.

BS: *What was the result?*

JMcQ: He was acquitted. The jury didn't want to send this poor guy to jail because he was helping this lady. His lawyer very cleverly argued, "Yep, yep, he administered this but, the state has no way of proving that that's what killed her. We contend that cancer killed her." The jury was looking for any excuse they could to acquit the guy, but he lost his privileges to practice in Manchester. He practiced in Exeter after that and where he was the hometown doctor. He put my shoulder back in after three of my girlfriends dislocated it.

Doc Quigg was a national reporter, but he came to Manchester to cover the story as did reporters from all over the country to cover this trial. William Loeb hosted an event for the out-of-town reporters at the Manchester Country Club. I just found this out recently going through some papers.

We had AP and UPI, and I would use the one who had the story first and the best lead. It came to a point where Loeb was having some financial difficulties, "We're going with one, but don't let it bother you or interfere with you that Nackey (Loeb) his wife was a Scripps."

Scripps owned UPI, which used to be United Press. There was a third wire service called International News Service, and that was Hearst's service, as in William Randolph Hearst. Hearst sold INS to UP, and they took the I as in International.

BS: *Any other thoughts about UPI?*

JMcQ: One of my jobs as managing editor of the Sunday News was to take William Loeb's directive of following national stories that he thought should be followed by the wires. He was especially interested in national stories that involved Jimmy Hoffa or the Kennedy family. He liked Jimmy Hoffa because Jimmy Hoffa bailed out the Union Leader. We would not have the Union Leader if it were not for the Teamsters.

Loeb had gone into Massachusetts in the late 1950s and started a paper to compete against the Haverhill Gazette. He did this at the invitation of some merchants. The other New England newspapers didn't like Loeb, who was pro-union. To retaliate, a consortium of newspapers purchased the Haverhill Gazette. Loeb sued the Haverhill Gazette and lost a judgment in court in something on the order of $3 million, which was a lot of money in the 1960s. He couldn't get a loan from the banks. They were all in bed with the other newspapers. He found the Teamsters and the Teamsters pension fund loaned William Loeb and the Union Leader the money to pay the judgment. We were then beholden to the Teamsters pension fund. We, meaning the corporation, were beholden for years and years to pay it back, and anytime we wanted capital, we had to get their okay if we were going to spend a bunch of money.

William Loeb was trying to get Jimmy Hoffa out of the slammer. He was the head of the Teamsters and convicted by Bobby Kennedy, who was the head of the investigation. Several books had shown that Kennedy had a 'get-Hoffa' squad, and he was not following the letter of the law when he got Hoffa after years of trying. Judge Earl Warren, from the U.S. Supreme Court, was one of the ones who said Kennedy gave Hoffa a rough deal, but Hoffa went to the slammer. Loeb spent a lot of time with investigative reporters trying to get Hoffa freed. When the big story would come out about Hoffa and Loeb didn't like the way the wires were playing it, he would call me to call the wires to tell them that they didn't know what the hell they were doing. Sometimes they changed the story or updated it, and sometimes they didn't. We were a big paper, and we were a big client for UPI, to which they paid attention to us.

BS: *UPI goes out of business, and that's how you lose it.*

JMcQ: UPI went under, and in the meantime, I think we had brought AP back before UPI went totally under. We did business with AP for several years, who always had the bigger New Hampshire operation. They were the richer wire service. UPI was always by the skin of its neck, making payroll, but as a result, they were a real hustling outfit, and they did a good job.

BS: *Will you give me random thoughts on what I have discovered about specific individuals? Let's start with Nackey Loeb?*

JMcQ: Meg Heckman is a journalism professor at Northeastern, and she's taught classes at the Nackey Loeb School, and she's writing a biography of Nackey Loeb. (Ms. Heckman's book *Political Godmother: Nackey Scripps Loeb and the Newspaper That Shook the Republican Party* has been published by Potomac Books, 2020). I've been sharing files with her. And, I am working on the history of the Union Leader and William Loeb. Meg Heckman is fascinated by Nackey Loeb in the Katharine Graham (Washington Post) role of a woman publisher who was a woman publisher, not just a figurehead. Meg, she had to hit me up by the side of the head because she asked me about doing this. I thought, silly girl, it's William Loeb that's the story, not Nackey Loeb. And then, I started going through the correspondence with Ronald Reagan and Nackey Loeb, and they were like pen pals. A lot of stuff. I don't think that Nackey Loeb ever met Katharine Graham or would certainly like her politics. Maybe like the fact that she took over from her husband, who killed himself.

BS: *What is your mandate for the Union Leader?*

JMcQ: It is the mission of the paper to afflict the comfortable and comfort the afflicted. That's what Finley Peter Dunne said in 1902 in Chicago. It's just to put out in print or electronic or any other form, news, and information that's helpful to the Granite State. That was Loeb's mission ever since he was in Vermont. He wanted to be in New Hampshire with the statewide newspaper. The "statewide newspaper" is a pretty old phrase, because where we are now one of only a handful of statewide newspapers. There used to be many statewide newspapers.

BS: *William Loeb vigorously backed Ronald Reagan. What did he see in him?*

JMcQ: William Loeb wrote his editorials and said what he saw in Ronald Reagan. He saw a guy who was a fierce conservative, anti-Communist, and could get elected. There were a lot of good conservatives that William Loeb backed but couldn't get elected dog catcher. Reagan did in 1980. He also ran in 1976 and didn't win the New Hampshire primary, but came very close to beating "Jerry the Jerk," excuse me, that's William Loeb's name for Gerald Ford in 1976.

BS: *Did Loeb develop the letters to the editor policy to run every letter received?*

JMcQ: William Loeb ran every letter to the editor from anywhere in the country. We had to stop that and finally convinced him that if you were from out of state, you had to be a subscriber. He was running letters from people who never saw their letter and never cared. They just liked the idea that somewhere their letter was printed. He would run letters from all over the country. We would run pages and pages of letters. Insane. Some of the people subscribed, but many learned about Loeb from the UPI or the AP.

**BS:** *May 17, 1957, a 14-year-old boy from New Hampshire wrote a letter chastising Loeb for calling the president of the United States "a stinking hypocrite, and have you seen your psychiatrist lately?"*

**JMcQ:** Who calls the president of the United States, when he wasn't calling him Dopey Dwight, a stinking hypocrite? Loeb was calling him a stinking hypocrite because of Joe McCarthy.

**BS:** *There was an editorial titled "Murdered," about Joe McCarthy.*

**JMcQ:** Loeb was a big backer and friend of Joe McCarthy. He also backed Thomas Dewey. Loeb backed a lot of people. Some of them got elected, and some of them didn't. Loeb was known for his 'letter to the editor' policy. It got crazy. We finally convinced him when you sent in a letter, and you weren't from New Hampshire, you had to send in the mailing label on your Union Leader. He didn't care how long they were. The best letters in the paper would start with "Listen you idiot and were followed by boldface type responses.

**BS:** *William Loeb described your father, BJ McQuaid, as absolutely fearless and colorful.*

**JMcQ:** Elias McQuaid, one of my father's brothers, was hired as a reporter and worked at the paper, and so did Joe McQuaid, not me, my uncle, Joe. They both worked for my father, BJ McQuaid. The Sunday News co-founder was a gentleman named Blair Clark, and his name, thanks to me, still appears every Sunday in the masthead on the editorial page. I restored it. Blair Clark was Eugene McCarthy's campaign manager in 1968. He was president of CBS News and the editor of the Nation.

**BS:** *BJ worked for AP.*

**JMcQ:** No, never. AP might have carried the Chicago Daily News dispatches, but BJ didn't work for them. My dad started working here in the 1930s and then went to Chicago with Knox, who owned this paper and the Chicago Daily News. My dad went out there in the '30s and then became a war correspondent for the Chicago Daily News Foreign Service.

(Joe refers to a picture in his office with his father and a group of men at a long wooden table. "He's sitting there, that's Joseph Goebbels dining room.")

BS: *He witnessed the naval bombing in the Aleutian Islands, and for the South Pacific. BJ was cited by Navy and Marine commanders for bravery in covering close up major engagements. I mean, the Marines said he was a brave guy. Did he report on three theaters of war?*

JMcQ: My brother says four. He was in the Aleutian Islands for several months during the war. I don't want to say he was Ernie Pyle. He had a different style of doing a lot of reporting for hometown newspapers. He was working for the Chicago Daily News Service. They were trying to get the war into people's homes by interviewing the kids fighting the war. My father would say, "What's your name, son," and he was talking to privates and sergeants and lieutenants and captains and General Patton and General Montgomery.

BS: *He witnessed D-Day.*

JMcQ: He was in on D-Day plus one, meaning the day after D-Day. My brother contends that he was in on Omaha Beach. I think he might have been at Utah Beach. That would have been a real kick because this book that I wrote, *Cog Days*, about the Cog Railway was about a colonel who went in on Utah Beach, and my father knew that colonel. I'm not sure. But it was D-Day plus one, and he wrote about coming in. Ships are still blowing up left and right. Then, he went all the way across Europe right into Germany.

BS: *When BJ is out in Chicago, he got offered a job in Detroit?*

JMcQ: That's at the end of the war. Frank Knox died, and the Chicago paper had been purchased by John Knight, Knight Ridder. My father was told there was no job for him in Chicago. He could go work in Detroit, which was another Knight Ridder paper, and he wasn't interested in that.

BS: *He said, "I've been to Detroit and once is too much."*

JMcQ: That's something that I wrote.

BS: *But he said it?*

JMcQ: BJ told me that he thinks he got a raw deal from Knight because he was the bearer of bad news. When my father was still in Europe toward the end of the war, he got a cable from his boss telling him to go do the big guy a favor. John Knight wanted him to look up his kid, who was a lieutenant in the army in the war. By the time my father got there, the kid had been killed in an ambush. My father had to write the story and send the note home.

I wrote a two-part series once about something involving one of my other grandfathers, and I started by saying, "All the stories my father told me were true." It took me years to find out because I thought he was bullshitting me. For example, he shared a tent with John Huston when they were covering the Aleutians. I turn on the TV one day, and John Huston is talking about my father. Then he tells me he lost his job because he gave John Knight the bad news. I don't believe that, and then I pick up the official biography of John Knight, and there's my father listed on this page, and Knight gets the news on the golf course. So, two and two together. That's all going in my book.

BS: *Did he fly gliders?*

JMcQ: He flew gliders after he lost a leg to diabetes. Long before, he had been a pilot during World War II. People with diabetes cannot have pilot licenses. He found out in the mid-1960s, hey they're flying gliders down in Salem, and you don't need a license to fly a glider because there's no engine.

BS: *You just gotta land it.*

JMcQ: A guy took him up in a glider, and he learned how to do that, and he wrote about that. Then he lost a leg to diabetes and had to give up golf. How can you live without golf?

BS: *But then he took up fishing.*

JMcQ: He took up fishing by towing a big boat behind a little Datsun 240Z and backing the boat and the car into Lake Massabesic. It didn't work out well.

BS: *How would you describe Nackey Loeb?*

JMcQ: Geez, how do I describe Mrs. Loeb? She was a very generous, thoughtful, tough lady with a wicked sense of humor.

BS: *Did she love horses?*

JMcQ: Yes. The horse farm in Goffstown was her daughter's. It was a riding place called Upreach Therapeutic. That was her daughter Edie's. Mrs. Loeb had two daughters, and they were both accomplished equestrians, as was Mrs. Loeb. William Loeb didn't do that. He and Mrs. Loeb fly fished, and goose hunted in Canada and skied in Nevada, where they were legal residents. They also shot pistols and played tennis. They were very athletic. So, imagine that this lady in the car accident gets paralyzed from the neck down. He gets thrown clear. She gets paralyzed. I never heard an angry word from this woman with all that she has to bear. She would call me a couple of times a week. "What's going on?" I'd start complaining about this or that, and what the Christ do I have to complain about? She never complained.

Her grandfather was a famous newspaperman, and so was her father. His name was Bob Scripps. He was the head of Scripps after his father. EW Scripps, the old man, died on his yacht off the coast of Africa. And, then I read somewhere, and I knew it must be wrong because it said Robert Scripps died on his yacht.

BS: *How many yachts are there?*

JMcQ: For Scripps, there were plenty. William and Nackey were also good sailors. I was talking to Mrs. Loeb and said, "Hey Mrs. Loeb, they must have this wrong. They said your father died on a yacht, too." She said, "He did." I said, "Your grandfather died on a yacht, and your father died on a yacht. I got some advice for you, Mrs. Loeb, stay the hell off boats." She liked that.

BS: *Someone described her as a real soldier in regard to her injury.*

JMcQ: She is quoted as saying, "God doesn't give you any more than he thinks you can handle." As I said, she never complained. She was in a wheelchair, and she would zip down on the sidewalk in front of the

Union Leader on Amherst Street like crazy. You'd try to keep up with her. It wasn't motorized. She would do it on her own. She had a van hooked up with an elevator, and she would hook herself in, and away we'd go. Dick Becker usually drove her here. She would come in once a week for meetings, which was four times more often than William Loeb. He came to New Hampshire once a month for meetings. She came every week. Then she moved up here, so it was easier.

BS: *I read that she was talking to a class, and she was asked to talk about personal success in newspapers. She said, "Personal success in newspapers came to her by falling in love with the right guy and marrying him." When I read that, I realized they had a real love relationship.*

JMcQ: He was devoted to her. That was his third wife.

BS: *Her second husband.*

JMcQ: Yes. I was interviewing her one day on some anniversary, and it occurred to me, ask her, "What the hell did you want to do as a kid?" She said, "I wasn't sure, but one thing I knew I didn't want to do was be in the newspaper business. And I married a newspaper guy."

BS: *I thought that this was a lovely relationship. They spoke the same newspaper language. When she passed, and you became publisher, how did you feel about taking over the reins of the publisher?*

JMcQ: She made me the publisher of the Union Leader before she passed. I've just had dumb luck my entire life in this business. It's like somebody's been watching out for me, and every few years before I had a chance to think about getting bored and doing something different, I got another job here. I'm the office boy. I'm a sports reporter. I'm covering the Manchester Yankees. I'm a full-time reporter and because my old man wants me to have Mondays off so I can play golf with him. I'm not only a reporter, but I'm a photographer and combo man. I come home one night, and I bring the paper home because he's ill. I'm not the Sunday editor. I'm just a reporter, and I bring the paper home. He spends an hour swearing and yelling at me about what's in the paper. One night I say, "Hey, don't yell at me. I'm not the editor." I thought I heard him say as I'm leaving his room, "Well, I can fix that too." The next week I was about to sit down at my reporter's desk, and one of the editors came over to me and said, "No, you don't sit there anymore. Your father says you sit over here." Now I'm the Sunday editor at 22 or something. And then my father dies. I'm 27, and I become the managing editor. Then Paul Tracy's wife calls me up at two in the morning one day and says that he's dead of a heart attack. I became the editor in chief. A few years later, Dick Becker retired, and that one I told Mrs. Loeb and her daughters, "You don't need to look anywhere. I will be your general manager. I can do this job." I wasn't surprised. I was pleased that she decided that I would be the publisher when she stepped down.

BS: *I understand the Cog Railway gift shop banned your book on the Cog Railway. Why?*

JMcQ: My agent up there says they are now selling it. I was very upset about that because now I've got to change my speech. I think somebody thought that my book (*Cog Days: A Boy's Life and One Tragic Summer on Mt. Washington*), that it was too soon. Fifty years after the accident that killed eight paying passengers. I went up there a month ago to give a talk at the Omni Mount Washington Resort. I drove up to the Cog, but the gift shop wasn't open yet, and so I couldn't tell if it was in there or not. But I did see a mama and three little cubs coming back down to the base.

BS: *How do you feel about the name Union Leader coming off the building as a result of the sale of the property?*

JMcQ: It didn't bother me. Things change. Although it was a little twinge, I would be happier if we were still on Amherst Street. The technology was not quite at the point of having satellite technology. It was back in the day when we'd say, "What do you mean we're not going to see the paper when it gets out. It's going to be five miles from us." Now it's 35-40 miles.

BS: *Brendan McQuaid is now the president of the New Hampshire Union Leader. Your son.*

JMcQ: Brendan's had quite a few jobs, not on the news side. He was a security guard. He was the office boy. He knows all the technical stuff. He went away to C-SPAN. He went to law school but didn't like it.

BS: *Can you explain the New Hampshire spirit? Is it explainable?*

JMcQ: Well, it's on the front-page tomorrow. There's bourbon touched with a beaver scent. That's a New Hampshire spirit. *The* New Hampshire spirit? The live free or die state is just so small geographically and population-wise, but it has this hellacious huge New Hampshire legislature with 424 people. That's great because they can't get anything done. There's no way they can do anything. That's what you want in a legislature. We pay them a hundred bucks, whether they are worth it or not.

Live free or die. I walk a lot, and I walk by John Stark 's homestead by his front door. The house is no longer there, but the steppingstone is there. I know down there is his grave, along with Molly Stark. And I know across the road is another road, Bennington, this little, tiny street. There aren't six people who know why it's called Bennington.

BS: *And you are one of them?*

JMcQ: It's from Bennington, Vermont. Stark had quit the continental army because he was fed up taking orders from the stupid congress. He came home here, and congress is all in a panic because the Hessians and General Johnny Burgoyne are coming down from Canada. If they link up with Cornwallis, America is toast. They send a message to Stark and Stark says, "I'll do it, but I'm not working for you guys I'm working for the people of New Hampshire." He raises an army with cannon, and he marches them by foot from here to Vermont in like three days. The stupid Hessians go into Bennington because they need shoes, and they shouldn't have gone in. He's got a trap for them. Stark beats these guys.

Stark was one of Rogers' Rangers in the French and Indian war. He was a tough guy. He got kidnapped by the Indians, Stark did. They make you run a line with Indians on both sides with tomahawks to whack at you. He, rather than just trying to run through, hits the first one and hits the second one, zigzags, and the chiefs are very impressed. They gave him his freedom. He was a New Hampshire man.

BS: *I talked to John Harrigan about you. John was a former columnist for the Union Leader. You and he were friends. He wrote a column, Woods, Water & Wildlife, for the Union Leader for over 40 years.*

JMcQ: John Dennis Harrigan, geez, you'll talk to anyone if you talked to Harrigan. At South Hill? Did he tell you about the big furnace, the big trees he puts in the furnace, the hummingbirds?

BS: *We saw a hummingbird.*

JMcQ: And the dog, Millie, the fierce Millie was there? What did Harrigan have to say?

BS: *He said that you're a good news guy, one of the best, and you love New Hampshire and all it stands for. He was a pallbearer at your father's funeral.*

JMcQ: He worked for BJ. I nominated him for the Pulitzer Prize. His sister and I nominated him for the article on the Colebrook killings at Harrigan's newspaper. His sister was a newspaper person down in New York, and her husband was too. Harrigan was a pallbearer at BJ McQuaid's funeral, as was Hemorrhoid, Harrigan's name for Dirk Rumenapp, former executive vice president of the Union Leader, as was John Hammond.

BS: *John's sister just retired from Newsday.*

JMcQ: She's the one holding the microphone into which Muskie is crying. It's a small state. We had a lot of fun together and played a lot of poker with John and Dirk and Fat Man and John's younger brother Peter who died of a heart attack out in California. He was working for a paper out there. Fat Man was R. Warren Pease. His kid runs one of our competitors. He was an investigative reporter for us, and he worked on the Sunday News. He had a little tummy. He was a gunner on a ship in World War II and was very proud of putting up mission symbols. An officer comes over and says, "Who the hell shot down one of our planes?" It was Fat Man.

BS: *Harrigan said, "I was so lucky to be alive with William Loeb. He was so much fun."*
JMcQ: *William Loeb was in his prime when John was the outdoor writer for the paper, so Loeb had a special knack for him. William Loeb got a real kick out of life and newspapering and raising hell. He was interested in everything from tie flying to flying airplanes to sports. Loeb bombarded his editors with blue-bordered memos. Four or five secretaries were constantly going, which is why he generated so much paperwork.*

**BS:** *They were called WL Grams.*

**JMcQ:** He didn't call them that. Maybe we did. Do you know who William Loeb's godfather was and who his godson is?

**BS:** *Brendan is Loeb's godson.*

**JMcQ:** William Loeb was the godson of Teddy Roosevelt. Loeb had several godsons and Brendan is one of them.

Do you know the name Bruce Springsteen? John Hammond signed him to his first record contract. Do you know the name Bob Zimmerman AKA Bob Dylan? John Hammond signed him to his first contract. Do you know the name Billie Holiday? John Hammond signed her to her first contract. How about Bennie Goodman? John Hammond was a lifelong friend of my dad's. They were newspaper guys when they were kids in Maine at a newspaper there. John Hammond loved my dad and vice versa even though Hammond was a big liberal, as was Blair Clark. John Hammond put money into the Sunday News as did some lady from Massachusetts, and they had to give her nephew a job, Ben Bradlee.

**BS:** *That was a good hire.*

**JMcQ:** BJ and Loeb flew down to Washington to be on a show that Ben Bradlee and Martin Agronsky were to appear on as well about the Canuck letter and Watergate. The Canuck letter was a letter to the editor that William Loeb should not have run. That's why Muskie was crying in front of the paper. The thing was about his wife, and that was phony on the part of Muskie, saying that Loeb attacked his wife. We reprinted something that had been in Women's Wear Daily and reprised in Newsweek. He didn't go down to Fifth Avenue and start crying in front of Newsweek. He was losing traction up here to McGovern.

That happened in 1972. In 1960, the night before the general election a guy got up across the street from the Union Leader and said (McQuaid talks in a bad Massachusetts accent), "There may be a worse newspaper and a worse publisher in these United States than William Loeb and the Union Leader but if there are I can't think of them right now." He won. His name was Kennedy, John Kennedy.

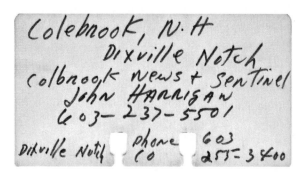

*Chapter 6*

---

John Harrigan—Rolodex Connection: Card on File

---

*Pulitzer Prize Finalist for Reporting of the Murder of his Editor and Dear Friend*

John Harrigan is the type of man who personifies the New Hampshire motto, "live free or die." He lives in Colebrook, New Hampshire, situated in Coos County in the Great North Woods region of the state. It is picturesque and the ideal place to hunt, fish, ride ATV's and above all, get away from it all. From the center of town, you hang a right and follow a steep, long dirt road to the top of a hill. You'll find Harrigan there on the 165 acres that he logs and acts as the "good steward of the land." Hummingbirds visit the feeder on the farmer's porch. The porch faces the view of the mountains that were renamed for Vickie M. Bunnell, the woman he loved.

Talking to Harrigan is like riding a roller coaster. It's fast and dips and turns quickly. Yet worth the ride. Before we get to the tragedy that he is known for, we talk about loons and bobcats, plutons and plebiscites, replacement hips, and always—newspapers.

On August 19, 1997, Carl Drega turned his decade's long-burning grudge against local government and law enforcement into outright murder. The toll that day included two state police officers, the editor of the Colebrook News & Sentinel, and a local judge with whom John was having a love affair. Publisher Harrigan was called away just minutes before Drega arrived armed to kill. The judge was shot as she ran and fell dead in the middle of the road.

I drive four hours north of my home in New Hampshire to Colebrook. I am terrified of heights, and the trip takes me through the Franconia Notch State Park. As you climb up through the mountains, you drive into the clouds. I have a steely grip on the steering wheel and am grateful that I cannot see the mountain tops. Even looking at a mountain gives me panic.

To read John Harrigan's essays, go to www.Newfoundlanding.com for the column, and there are archives of the papers

BS: *Harrigan, on crutches, has had hip surgery. He begins by commenting that I made it.*

JH: Terra incognito—some people get concerned and a little bit afraid. This is no kidding. They worry they've come too far, have gone by it. You actually have a situation in which people submit for teaching jobs and refuse to go any further. The school board up here has an opening for a teaching position. They advertise and, of course, they go through the SEA and many various job posting places. The school board gets a call from 'Fred Smith," and he's got an interview set for seven in the evening because they are working people. It's always going to be an evening appointment when they are hiring, which they try to do before school ends in the spring. They'll call and set the interview up for 7:00 at night, and "Fred Smith" is told it's a 3-hour drive from Manchester. He gets directions, and they give their home phones in case there's a problem. One of the school board members will get a call at home, and it'll be from "Fred Smith" saying, "Hi. I'm at Franconia Notch. How far am I?" And they're told, "You're about halfway." The person says, "Halfway! I'm not coming. Count me out."

BS: *I believe it. You hit that notch, and you can't see twenty feet in front of you.*

JH: Everything often changes with the weather above the notch. It's lowery with no breaks. I haven't seen a break in the clouds. "Lowery" is still very much in use here, as are a good number of old English words and phrases. Our ways from the waves of settlers some of the old words and accents survived generations moving up the rivers, and in our case, they came up from the Gulf of Maine, most of them. They bought land up here, and they brought with them some of the old sayings. I grew up with the high-country people, higher than this, and they still had this in their vernacular. Fetch, for instance, you don't hear often but is still very much in use up here. "Can't abide by this." That is the strongest term.

I'm not used to hitting these keys, he says, referring to his new I-Phone. I'm just learning to run this thing. I've only had it for three weeks. I can text, but I don't. I don't know why I'm so stubborn about getting into that aspect of the thing, but I am. Everybody tells me it's a great phone. This comes after years of my family just totally out of patience with me because I had an old flip phone, a Jitterbug, as advertised on TV. Jitterbug was a very good choice and was desirable and inevitable. Here the big cell phone surge didn't hit until about five years ago.

About 2012-2013 is when some key towers were put in, and huge dead zones were eliminated over the North Country. Word quickly spread that those were now active. That's when cell phones went through the roof. Couldn't keep them on the shelves. That's when I saw people downtown walking around with the phone plugged to their ear. And it was a sea change.

BS: *An s-e-e change?*

JH: An s-e-a change is when unusually high tide comes in. It's destructive, a major turning point event. That was the first time since the advent of the telephone that communications had been put into the hands of the people — nothing like it ever in what passes for civilization.

BS: *You look the very same as the picture that was used with your column when you were writing for the Union Leader. I heard you got two new knees. My husband had one done.*

JH: I got two new knees at the same time. Here's the rationale because you're on board. I did the research because I had one bad knee, and I knew the other one was okay, but not for long. One of the stories I kept bumping into in my research was, "Joe Schmo" has to have two knees done. Wife, family, friends all say, "Oh, you can't stand the pain of two at once. Get one done." Always the easy way out. They talk him into it, and he goes and gets one done. Then somebody asks him, "Joe, when are you gonna get the second knee done?"

I'm going to use language I don't usually use, and Joe says, "The second knee? No fucking way. Are you stupid?" The pain is so bad, and "Joe Schmo," having been through one knee, never gets the other knee done. My brother-in-law, my sister Mary's husband, is built like Hoss Cartwright; a strong, big guy and his knees have taken a lot of punishment. He's gotta get 'em both done. He got one done. He listened to everybody. I call them the Care Bears, cause the Care Bears are always out there, from the book. The Care Bears, all the sensitive, loving, caring people talked him into waiting, doing one, and that's his answer if he's doing the other one, "No fucking way!"

BS: *It's a miracle cure.*

JH: If I had known that I couldn't run on these knees, my immediate question would have been, do you have a supermodel? Give me the Cadillac because I was a long-distance runner for almost 40 years, not a jogger, a runner, and I was three inches taller. I was almost 5'11," and now I'm 5'8" because of gravity.

BS: *And now you have a temporary hip?*

JH: It's called a spacer. I fell down and smashed a hip back here at the beginning of the bird season around October 1st. I smashed the hip, and I live alone. Millie was out (his 13-year-old miniature poodle). The phone was over there (across the kitchen from where he fell). I was here (pointing at a place on the kitchen floor near the counter).

I did damage control as I was lying on the floor with a smashed-up hip. I had to get to my feet, and I didn't have any crutches around. I used this counter, and there were crutches over there in the corner from a previous injury. I managed to use the table for support and pulled myself up to my feet and got over to my phone and called the ambulance. I got over in the corner and got the crutch and went to the door and got Millie because it was cold, and she's pushing thirteen now, poor little dog, and I couldn't leave her out with her little plastic nose.

I went down to Concord Hospital. The reason I chose that hospital is Concord Orthopedics is there. I'm a big believer in that outfit. One of their surgeons did a great job of putting a hip in for me, and unfortunately, during the operation, something hitched a ride in.

**BS:** *An infection?*

**JH:** I'm being told three or four weeks later that I had an infection, and it was bonded to the apparatus of the new hip. It adheres itself to something and builds a tent much as a ladybug does. They told me it had to come out, and I fought it fiercely. I was five days in the hospital, and I started walking on day five, and on day six walked to my neighbor's house, which is half a mile or so. I was doing great and then to be told that you have to lose that. They could not get the infection out. We tried getting it out. They opened me up again and flushed the area with antibiotics. Of course, by then, I was on the heaviest antibiotic you could take and still didn't work.

**BS:** *Fight the infection and keep the hip.*

**JH:** There's a process, a strategy for that called keeping something in check, abatement. I tried this process, but then the more we met with people, the more they said this was folly. It could get in the bloodstream, and I could get sepsis, and it could kill me. Finally, we had a meeting, and I saw three people right in a row, and I asked the final questions of each one. Would you, if it were your mother, would you advocate for them to keep the hip? One right after the other said no, to not keep the hip. It wasn't the pain; it was they had done a good job on the hip. I went in and had the hip taken out, and so that was three surgeries. The first one was to replace the busted hip — the second one to flush it out, and the third to take it out.

**BS:** *How long do you keep this temporary?*

**JH:** I'm hoping that the lab results I'm waiting for will be good and hope we get the green light. The next surgery is scheduled for the end of June, the last Thursday. It's called a spacer. I can put 30 percent of the weight on my foot, and I have to be careful about how I move around. And I got to tell you, adjusting to life on crutches 24/7 is not an easy thing, and I have a deeper respect and feeling for people who have to use these and are never going to get out of them. I am getting out of them and somehow get a new hip. The spacer lives up to its name and holds the hip in place. I can move my leg and control just can't put regular body weight on it.

(Note: John has since had a total of five operations to get his hip fixed. He says he is better and still working on his recovery.)

BS: *The coffee John has made is ready. He says, "I make ice cream out of my coffee," and adds French Vanilla Baileys coffee creamer and three heaping teaspoons of sugar to his cup. I ask how long have you lived here?*

JH: 1994. I guess it was, and it was nothing like it is now. I built all these barns, and there's a sheep barn and a hay barn.

BS: *How did you get to be a publisher?*

JH: I inherited the News and Sentinel from my parents. At one time, I owned the Coos County Democrat in Lancaster and started a direct mail tabloid called the Northern Beacon.

BS: *The News and Sentinel is a third-generation newspaper. Karen (his daughter) is the current owner of the News & Sentinel.*

JH: She's a Nazi. I'd no more work for that woman. She takes after her mother for beauty and is as ruthless as I am or have been.

BS: *What about Joe McQuaid? You worked for him.*

JH: Joe McQuaid and I were fast friends, for years and years, I was a columnist for him for a long time. and the parting was not easy, nothing major.

BS: *Did you and he have a fight?*

JH: It was time for me to go. Times were changing, and the paper was changing in ways that I was not happy with but fully understood. The Union Leader/NH Sunday News were both having to change to meet the challenges of the times. And it was time. I had been writing the column for 37 years at that time. I had a great run, and that established my name statewide because it was a statewide newspaper. Then I got into the radio. I had a great time working for Joe, absolutely the best news guy I ever bumped into. He takes after his father, BJ McQuaid.

BS: *He's a tough guy.*

JH: He takes after his father. (He makes a comment that he asks me not to repeat.)

BS: *If you want me to keep something off the record, I will.*

JH: Off the record is a movie term that I never use. It came from a movie called The Front Page. There are two things reporters should not use: one is 'for background only,' meaning that you can use the information, but you can't say where it came from, and the second is 'not for attribution,' which means you can use the quote. Someone gives you a juicy quote like 'the president's lost his head,' you can't say who said that, but you can say that it was a 'senior White House aide,' I love these nuances of newspapers.

BS: *You can't burn your bridges, so you want all those sources to respect you and know you will keep your word. You have a couple of cards in the Rolodex.*

JH: The Rolodex is a fascinating idea for a book, and I'm in a book family. My brother-in-law has published several books and wrote the history of Motown, Peter Benjaminson. Nobody had done it. He was amazed. He did that and has had several books since. *Death in the Afternoon* was about the demise of afternoon dailies. I was fascinated by it as I started my work with an afternoon daily. It was at the Nashua Telegraph.

BS: *I worked for the Telegraph too.*

JH: I worked from '68 to '72 and went straight to the Sunday News. They called me. You love it when they call you. I had to become a union member to stay there and didn't really want to. If I wanted to, I could have made a crusade about it. I felt it should be an open shop. Like all unions, they are mere shadows. This is my fiftieth year of newspapering. I'm still writing.

BS: *Wow, your fiftieth year. And some say newspapers are dead.*

JH: They're not. The good newspapers are making it. People still want to turn to something with a gatekeeper, and there's no gatekeeper on most of the stuff on the internet. You need to be selective and know what sources are involved in the story. Unfortunately, I have to use the word 'consumers,' a lot of people aren't savvy enough to figure it out. "Wait a minute, where did this story come from?" Well, it came from the United Arab Emirates. People are looking nostalgic for media that have some sort of gatekeeper, editor.

The only medium that does that in a backtracking method so reliably is print. The printed newspaper is the medium for accountability, not to mention readability. God help me with some of the junk I see.

BS: *I love newspapers and will always read them. I started in 1973 and worked for Gannett.*

JH: I didn't work for Gannett, but I got a job offer from Gannett out in New Mexico. I was offered a good job. Just by happenstance, my wife, at the time, had some business in Albuquerque. For the hell of it, I just made what salespeople call a cold call. I called the publisher of the New Mexican. I think it could have been Santa Fe; anyway, I cold-called him and said, "Hey, I'm a newspaperman from way back, and I'm here and my wife's throwing money around down on Main Street. Can I come up and get a tour of your place? I'm particularly interested in your press room." He says, "It's lunchtime almost. Want to go out for lunch?" What the hell, I figured it was gonna be a 45-minute lunch and throw down a beer and then rush back to work. It wasn't. It was the most enjoyable lunch I ever had, languorous, stretched into more than two hours.

BS: *It sounds like a lunch with two people who had a lot in common.*

JH: Subsequently, he called me up and wanted to know if I wanted to work for Gannett. I would have been a union buster. In some ways, I was suited for what he said were 'problem towns,' towns where they were having a hard time establishing itself. I don't know if it was going to be a union thing necessarily, but it would have been a hard situation, and it meant that I would continually be put in a wound of some sort and try to heal it. And they'd yank me out of there and put me in another town where they had some problems. I could see nothing but strife, plus moving a lot, and it would be hard on my family. The money was unbelievable.

BS: *I read your Union Leader column, "Woods, Water and Wildlife," every Sunday.*

JH: Who would think that somebody in advertising would be faithful to an outdoor column? I'm 71, and I never thought I'd make it. I'm astounded to be sitting here and saying that because most of my adult life, I thought I was going to bite the dust at 65. I had a premonition. My dad died at 69. Much of my family died in their mid-sixties. I had worked myself pretty hard. Among other things, I moved a press with my chief pressman from Rochester to Lancaster.

BS: *Did you move an entire press?*

JH: We did all the work of jackhammering it out. It used to print the Rochester Courier. We jackhammered it out and pushed it on steel roller bars. They were solid steel and were maybe an inch in diameter, and we had thirty or forty of them. You'd sweep the floor up pretty well, and you laid down a few, say six, and then you use pry bars or whatever you have at your disposal. We had a small electric machine that was used to move freight around inside the building. We didn't have forklifts. This machine couldn't lift anything, but it could push, so we used it to push the press from its former place onto these rollers until the machine could go no further. It had a boom at the top. We had to push it by hand. It was four units and a folder on the same story as the loading dock. We pushed them by hand, out to the loading dock where we had a flatbed truck. The press weighed 27 tons. The folder on top of it had to be a good five tons. We pushed everything out, and a crew loaded it onto the flatbed and took it on up to Lancaster.

BS: *Did they install it for you?*

JH: No. The crew got it to the loading dock, and we had to put it into a rough position. We hired a guy from Goss Community Press out of Chicago. It's pretty dicey stuff. I helped with the lining up phase. I was at the number four-unit, and he was up at the folder with a laser, and the guy would say, "Give it another tap." I had like an eight-pound sledgehammer, and I'd give the unit just a tap, just a little tap. He'd say, "Okay, hold it," and he'd say, "Give it another one." That's how we lined them and trimmed them and leveled them. But I'm getting off the track. You have to stop me.

In my office upstairs, I can look right out the window at the range of mountains over in Columbia called the Blue Mountain plutons by the geologists. It's a generic term in geology for a massive rock outcropping. And there it is this incredible series of mountains in an unknown corner of New Hampshire. The pluton means a massive piece of a ledge. Geologists were interested in it about twenty or thirty years ago. They wanted to store radioactive material there because the Blue Mountain pluton is and was one of the most stable geological formations in the world. And the U.S of A. 'govmint' had a plan to make these incredible tunnels and put radioactive waste in there. The public got a murmur up here, and, of course, it didn't happen.

BS: *You were a Pulitzer finalist. What did that feel like?*

JH: I was a Pulitzer Prize first finalist. That's right within a whisker of getting it. I found out later my sister Susan nominated the paper. She was active in a whole string of dailies. I call her Hanoi Jane because of her politics. She just retired at Newsday. Susan Harrigan.

BS: *Why did you call her Hanoi Jane?*

JH: She's to the left of Che Guevara, for goodness sake because of her politics. She found out through friends that the Pulitzer people had no idea what we had gone through that night here. And I was told by a couple of people that knew people that if they had a better grasp of what went on here, we would have had it. As it stands, we got beat out by the LA Times for Christ's sake, and they had 250 reporters in their newsroom at that time. We had three, not even — two in the newsroom. We had a bunch of stringers.

I had not a clue to know how to run a newspaper when I started my career. I learned fast. You have to know everything about everything. Or at least a little bit about everything. I ran my own press, which was another oddity because very few publishers in the United States have ever run their own press. Once my chief pressman and I had trained a crew, I didn't have to run the press. I put my own paper out. We published weekly.

We went to press Tuesday night, but very soon after I got the press in, we began to print other papers. Eventually, we printed my parent's paper, which we competed with. The Coos County Democrat competed with The Sentinel. My father and mother owned it jointly.

BS: *As they say, you have ink in your blood.*

JH: Look at Euler's Circle. One of the same I remember from my geometry course (he draws circles on the paper.) Your first circle goes like this, your second circle like this and the third like this. And so on until you wind up with a circle that goes like this. This being Lancaster and this up here being Colebrook. Colebrook's circulation only went about halfway to Lancaster. Its circulation was from Stratford north.

BS: *That means there was minimal overlap in circulation.*

JH: Correct. The chief areas being Groveton, Stratford, the Vermont towns of Bloomfield, and Brunswick. Those areas overlapped. But we were coming into their backyard far more than they were coming into ours. We had a big push to make the Coos County Democrat live up to its name after I bought it. The Lancaster paper had very little north country news in it. I did this with my circulation. I made a major push to go head to head with my folks and The Sentinel. The nice thing is they didn't get hurt by this. My dad and I used to joke about it over lunch. People who had always bought the news from the Sentinel now they were buying the Democrat because they wanted to see what the Sentinel didn't have. They kept on reading the Sentinel. They bought both because they had a hell of a lot of fun going home and looking the Sentinel over and then saying, "Now what's the Democrat have?"

BS: *They knew it was father versus son.*

JH: And that was the big yuck. Everybody knew we were competing. It was great. We had more fun during those years. I would never tell my father what we were working on. In fact, they broke down one time. I forget exactly the reason, an electrical problem. They were dead in the water, and it was a Monday morning. They called us. They realized they were in trouble. They asked me if they could come down if they could use our typesetting and paste-up facilities to put their paper together. And I said, of course. Newspapers have a rich tradition of helping each other in times of stress, even bitter enemies.

In fact, I lent my press motor one time to a bitter rival over in Berlin. Couldn't stand the bastard. Can't think of his name now. I gave him my press motor to use while he was getting his motor rebuilt. Mother and father brought their paper down, and it's all normally in their heads, and they put it together in my newsroom using my typesetting facilities but their own paste-up people.

We had a big curtain set up in the newsroom so we couldn't see what they were doing. In paste-up, we had some kind of blockade made, so when the paper was being laid out and pasted up, and we were waxing and cutting and pasting, we couldn't see what they were doing. And they couldn't see what we were doing. The two crews worked side by side when the negatives were being shot. Dad and his darkroom people went in, and my darkroom person had to help because there's alchemy involved. Right up to the press, we never saw their front page.

BS: *How do you like the idea of stories from the Rolodex?*

JH: I'm going to tell my writing friends about this. Jeff Fair is one of my writing friends. He's down here doing some loon work on the Richardson Lake Chain in Maine. He came down from Alaska, where he lives, to do biological survey work on the chain, the Umbagog, Richardson Lake, Mooselookmeguntic Lake. There are others I've forgotten. There are seven lakes. Jeff Fair is a writer of great New Hampshire renown because he led the loon preservation committee for about a dozen years. Largely responsible for the comeback of the loon in New Hampshire. He's one of my best friends. And oddly enough, my other best friend, if you can have two, is John Lanier, who used to be a wildlife biologist as Jeff is. During his career, he was largely responsible for the comeback of the peregrine falcon.

BS: *It's okay. Tell me about your family.*

JH: Obviously, there's no woman in the house. I've been through two marriages. I'm not through the second one, no papers have passed, but I've been on my own for several years, at least three. I have three kids, Karen is the oldest, and she runs the News & Sentinel. She worked for other newspapers and came up to help after the shootings, during that crisis and really didn't want to go anywhere else. She was working for Joe McQuaid, and he lent her to me. I have never pried beyond that. Except she said that, and I believe he continued to pay her salary even though she wasn't doing her regular work for him. She was helping out here. We got the paper out that night, but the shock set in the next day for the crew. Getting the paper out was a big deal. And once we had reached that objective, the air went out of the bag the next day. The stuffing had been kicked right out of us. We lost our editor, Dennis Joos, and we lost Vicky. He was an incredible guy, very funny. He tried to save her to save everybody. The gunman was there, and he was shooting when Dennis Joos came out the door. He was the last one out, and if I had been there, I would have been behind him. A phone call saved my life.

My office was the furthest from the back door. It was in the extreme southeast corner of the building. I would have been behind Dennis, and when he came out, shots were being fired. Vicky fell. Dennis thought the guy was going to shoot the whole crew, and he went for him without hesitation. People throw the word hero around all the time, but Dennis, without a moment's hesitation, launched himself at that guy and who was taller than him and outweighed him by fifty pounds. He had a sidearm handgun and the semi-automatic he was using.

BS: *He launched himself at the gunman.*

JH: Without even thinking, Dennis had to save his crew. I would have been right behind him.

What would I have done? I don't know, but I hope that I would have. To say the least, it haunts me. But I wasn't there. A phone call saved my life.

BS: *What was the call?*

JH: One of the key paste-up people at the Democrat got a call that her father had just dropped dead down in Massachusetts. She had to leave on the fly. This was Tuesday, and they were pasting up the inner pages of the paper. She got the phone call that her father had just dropped dead, so she dropped everything and ran for the door. The editor, Gene Ehlert, called me up and said, "Nancy had to leave. Could you come down and help us out?" This happened every now and then. I could do every job in the newspapers. If somebody was shorthanded, I could step in. I ran and left a note for Bunny (Bunny Bunnell), Vicky's father because we were going to go fishing that afternoon. He was my best friend before I knew there was a Vicky. She came later. I went in to tell Vicky that I was going down-country. I gave her a hug, and that was the last time I had a chance to hug her.

I flew down the highway in my dad's great big Lincoln I had inherited that was a city block long and took two tugboats to park. He liked big cars. I burned the road up and hadn't been down at the Democrat ten minutes when the scanner went wild. It was going crazy. Within five minutes, we knew roughly what had happened. And on the way out, I said, "It was that bastard." I can't think of his name because I don't use his name. "Drega." I said right to everybody as I was going, "It's that bastard, Drega." He said he was going to kill her. She was in fear for her life for months and months.

BS: *Was there no way to anticipate it?*

JH: He had made threats and yelled obscenities at her from his truck in downtown Colebrook.

BS: *She was a judge.*

JH: She was a district court judge but mainly a private attorney. She had a practice in the News & Sentinel building in the front. If you go down-town, you'll see the Sentinel, the first right after you cross the bridge. It's the first building on the right. And there's a plaque that we put up when she established her practice. It is still there under my dad's.

BS: *There are reports that you were going to be married. Is that accurate?*

JH: We had split up for a little while, but we were getting back together. We realized we really belonged together. We were in the process of that when this thing happened. We were treading very carefully. She knew that I was working on getting free from my situation and doing whatever I had to do. She was doing the same.

BS: *How old is Millie the dog? I was surprised to see a poodle.*

JH: Not my kind of dog. I used to have Labs. She came here under convoluted circumstances. She didn't really have a future home, and my then wife's daughter had her and had to move to a new apartment. She wound up here. No one ever asked me about this. This dog just showed up at my house. To say the least, I wasn't that happy. Not because of the dog, but because of the disrespect that was shown. Now I wouldn't part with her. I couldn't imagine life without her. To show you how ruthless I can be, Joe McQuaid has nothing on me when it comes to this kind of stuff. I can be ruthless when I have to be.

I don't like that side of me like killing off newspapers that were coming into my territory. I was ruthless. I killed three newspapers. But in the case of Millie, I rationalized, the human mind is great for rationalization, I rationalized that I couldn't and shouldn't take it out on the dog because it wasn't her fault. She doesn't know what's going on. She's just a dog. The dog wasn't going anywhere. I wasn't going to force the dog out in the cold. Then I said if the dog is going to be under my roof, it's going to be my dog. At that point, she was considered everybody's dog, the family dog. I embarked on a campaign to kidnap Millie and her affection. I embarked on this secret. Nobody knew. Millie knew because I love dogs. I began doing little things with her, making sure she was always with me when I went for a ride and giving her little treats, offering her a place for her to come up and sit by me, and you do this with eye contact. It took me about two to three weeks to steal her. She was my dog, and I was hers.

BS: *Do you still have Willy's Jeep?*

JH: The '47 and it was one of the things that I made a vow that I wanted. I think there were four things that I had picked out what I wanted in life — not very material. One was the jeep that was made the same year that I was. I learned to drive on a '48 up at Moody's, where I lived for the formative years of my life. I made a vow in early adulthood, and I had a meeting with myself, which I do every now and then, and one of the things I made a mental list that I wanted a jeep. I was living with Rudy and Joan Shatney. My parents had me go live with them when I was 12. And the second vow was a camp on a remote pond. And the third thing was lots of lands to work on so that I could see over the long term what some of the values I had learned could accomplish. And I have that, and I've done that.

I have about 165 acres here, and as evidence of that, I'm now just completing a logging job on the very same forest ground that we logged when I first moved here. We're doing the same kind of job that I laid out back in 1994 or '95 using the same basic approach in the same area. We just logged it again. In 25 years, I'm not going to make it, but whoever else is going to be the temporary steward of this place can log it again if they use the same principles. I had five things in mind that I always stuck to, and here we are doing the same thing on this resilient forest we live in. It's all self-regenerating. I had the satisfaction of doing that. How many people have a big piece of land that they can do some of this stuff on and see the results? I'm a lucky guy. Most of these buildings were not here.

BS: *What do you think of the phrase live free or die?*

JH: I love the phrase live free or die, but most people don't know the second part of it, which is, death is not the worst of evils.

BS: *Tell me about William Loeb.*

JH: I was so lucky to be in the game when William Loeb was still active. It was so great to work for his outfit when he was still pretty much in his prime. He was so much fun. Like Mel Thompson, the former Governor. Now, did I agree with either of those guy's politics? No, not necessarily. In most cases, no. That's not the important thing. They were interesting people. They did crazy things. Some of them were abhorrent to many people and me. Still, it was like having had a chance to know Boss Tweed of Tammany Hall. Teddy Roosevelt. I wished to hell I had known that guy. I was there for Loeb, and he was such a character and such a guy.

I knew that I was going to be fine with him because he knows my stuff. Right away, I hadn't been on the job two days, and I got my first WL Gram. (William Loeb Gram). That's what we used to call them. They came on half sheets with a blue border all around them. And he'd send them around to people. He knew my family name, too, because my dad had been active with the Hugh Gregg campaign for governor. Loeb had supported Wesley Powell. The Harrigan's had been known to the Loeb people way back because my dad ran Hugh Gregg's second and successful campaign for governor. He ran twice for governor, and the second time he got it. Dad ran the first campaign and was like the assistant manager for the second one. Loeb knew my family name, and he knew my folks ran the newspaper up here, which he called the Pipsqueak Press. The weeklies never forgave them for that. He used that phrase one time on a frontpage editorial when he was mad at the weeklies for supporting someone he didn't, and he was irked. Back when the weeklies supported somebody that he loathed.

BS: *Trapping bobcats. You're against that.*

JH: I was vehemently against that particular proposal because of the overwhelming public sentiment that we should not be hunting and killing bobcats. It was about eight to one. And, I had to because Fish and Game was so out of touch with the public. The bobcat was an example of how the Fish and Game Department was so out of touch with the public. And Joe McQuaid, on that issue, was totally out of touch with his readership. The newspaper thought that we should have the season. We founded the NH Coalition about that time a few months before the bobcat controversy came up. Chris Schadler and I formed it months before that, in secret, because we wanted to keep it close to the vest for a while. Then the bobcat thing came along, and we fought it tooth and nail. We ultimately won because we packed the legislative hall. It was one of the two times I've seen the hall so packed to the rafters. I'll never forget the sight. I walked in there, and two-thirds of the legislative hall that is beautiful and vast is packed. It's really neat. It is the nation's oldest legislative chamber in which the originally intended body is still sitting.

We packed it, and the politicians could see that the people didn't want it. I hate making decisions by plebiscite because sometimes in the wildlife business, it's not the right way to go. I have to amend that with a comma or a semicolon and say that I also thought that it was wrong for hunters and hunting because it so devalued the worth of a bobcat. The bobcat has a value all its own. It's a part of the ecosystem, and we should not be killing them.

BS: *Woods, Water, and Wildlife—your column was great. You brought the woods to those who may never had the luck to see it and be in it.*

JH: It is kind of a Walter Mitty thing if you look at that way. He fantasized about himself in all these situations. And that's what people did. I loved that part of what I did, and I still do it. I'm still doing the same kind of column every week. This week's column is in my head.

BS: *Are you religious?*

JH: My church is out there. My hummingbirds are back. You can see that I'm on an ATV trail. I wanted you to see part of the view even though it's lowery. The Blue Mountain pluton has been renamed the Bunnell Mountain for Vicky. That's the tallest peak in the whole territory. It's a big mountain named Blue Mountain because it does look blue from a distance. Now it's Bunnell Mountain. It's an unknown little patch of New Hampshire. It's a big section of territory between Colebrook and Stratford, between Route 3 and Route 16. You could go over there with a pack on and spend the whole day in those mountains, go to the summit and not see another person. *A hummingbird comes to his feeder.* They are my hummingbirds. It's funny how people take ownership of them.

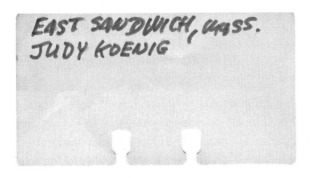

*Chapter 7*

---

## Judy Koenig—Rolodex Connection: Card on File

---

*Reporter/Photographer/Stringer*

In a male-dominated industry, I went looking through the cards for women and found a Rolodex card for Judy Koenig. I took a chance, called the number, and Judy answered. Judy Koenig is 83. She turned from being a nurse and mother, attending PTA and school committee meetings into a job at a local weekly newspaper. She learned the job along the way. That led to covering three murders, a devastating fire, and writing a political column for 17 years. She served eight years on the Board of Selectman and raised three boys, one of whom died when he was 27.

BS: *Judy. You are listed as a stringer for UPI. What articles did they use from you?*

JK: I pulled out my old portfolio I had; that's mostly my photography, but some of the stories were there. I had a story and photo I did, and there's a little clipping on it. I wrote "the Globe Magazine, UPI." So that must have been where it came from.

BS: *What was it about?*

JK: It was about a near-drowning down here at the Sandwich Marina. It was a great heroism story, two lives saved, and one was missing. I had the pictures and the story, and the Cape Cod Times picked it up. Then a fishing and boating magazine picked it up and then the Boston Globe.

BS: *And your byline is on it. That's big.*

JK: Yes, my byline is on it. It was fun.

BS: *How did you start in newspapers?*

JK: I started out in nursing. I was a licensed practical nurse and worked at the Community Hospital for several years. In Rutland, my boys were in elementary school. I started going to PTA meetings and went to school committee meetings. There was a newspaper in Holden called the Holden Landmark that was just getting on its feet. They asked if I would report on the school committee meetings. I had never taken a typing course, and I wrote out in longhand the first few stories and delivered them to Holden. I got a manual typewriter. Can you imagine? I learned to type the hunt and peck method. I gradually moved up to an electric typewriter and then a word processor.

BS: *What year did you start at the Holden paper?*

JK: That was in 1978. I was only working for them for about a year before we moved to Sandwich. I started writing in 1980 for the Sandwich Broadsider, which was started out by a couple here in town. It started in the basement of their house. I did a lot of reporting and photography for them. I worked for them until 1987 when I was elected to the board of selectmen.

BS: *Were you always a photographer?*

JK: I always liked photography, but I really got into it when I worked for the Broadsider. I loved doing it. I have a lot of nice black and white pictures. I tried doing my own developing but didn't have the patience for it. I took it to the paper, and they did the processing, and then I took the negatives and did my own enlargements. I had them done outside.

BS: *What kind of assignments did they send you on?*

JK: I did most everything. I got into some investigative reporting quite a bit. They would assign me to a few things. Mostly I picked things up on my own and ran it by the editor, of course, and went from there.

BS: *So, you used your experience from the other paper to get this job.*

JK: There were just the two of them that published the paper, and they had one advertising person, and they were trying to do a little bit of the reporting themselves. So, when I walked in, they sent me out on something right away, and it kind of steamrolled from there.

BS: *You walked in looking for a job, and the kids were in school? What did you work on?*

JK: I received an inside tip that our superintendent of schools, back in 1981, was in trouble legally. It turned out he was guilty of larceny and fraud in the school system. Nobody else had it. I broke it. The superintendent and the head of maintenance here both went to prison. I went to interview the superintendent at the prison. They told him he had a visitor. He came right out, took a look at me, turned around, and went back in. He didn't want to show his face that he did it.

BS: *What are some of the photographs that you remember taking?*

JK: There was a big, big fire; I don't remember when; maybe it was 1981 over at Scusset Beach. It got totally out of control, and I heard about it. The advertising person and I got into the middle of it. I've got several photos and did a big story, but while we were there, we got kind of locked in and couldn't get back out the way we came in. It circled around us a bit, but we got out.

BS: *Why did the ad person go with you?*

JK: There wasn't anybody else. We worked together and were friendly, and I said let's go and so off we went. We were kind of just friends. You know buddies. There were so few of us.

The paper changed hands along the way, but I kept on working for them. It went to MPG, a company in Plymouth. I continued to work for them under the Broadsider name and did a majority of the photos and quite a bit of journalism. I had to step down when I ran for selectman.

BS: *You said you were a columnist for 17 years.*

JK: I was elected three times for the board of selectmen and decided that was enough. In 1995, the Falmouth Enterprise contacted me. They were going to start a paper in Sandwich and asked if I would work for them. I had been doing a few columns for the old Broadsider, and they wanted to know if I would continue to do columns for the Enterprise. I did that for 17 years.

BS: *What was the focus of the column?*

JK: It was a lot of local politics and soft stories. It was weekly. I never worked for a daily.

BS: *Did you ever face any kind of discrimination at that time in your life?*

JK: Not in my work. When I was on the board of selectmen, there were some issues with men.

BS: *You would do your job, and it didn't matter you were a woman. What did your husband say about your career?*

JK: My husband was the most patient man, and he was proud. He would let me do my thing while he worked. His name was Emil. He was a physician, and he was a local doctor back in Holden for many years. He died several years ago. When we came here, he worked for the Barnstable County Hospital on staff there. His specialty was surgery. My work was never a problem. When I was a selectman, I was out many nights late. I don't think he was too happy with that.

BS: *Why did you become a selectman? And not selectwoman?*

JK: Selectman and selectwoman get debated over the years. They want to make it selectperson now in one of the towns down here. To me, it doesn't make any difference. It never was an issue. I was reporting on all kinds of things in town for seven or eight years. I went to all the selectman's meetings, school committee meetings, the board of appeals, the board of health all of those, and also some of the county meetings. I kinda knew all that was going on as a very familiar name and face in town. There were a lot of stories out there, and that's why I did it. I was in that position for eight years. I was elected three times and was the top vote-getter all three times.

BS: *Did you ever have any fights with constituents?*

JK: I got sued once for libel, but that was when I was writing a column. A local lawyer didn't like what I wrote about her when she was at a meeting. It was something like being a lawyer she should have known. I forget what the issue was and what the law said. She claimed ignorance of it, and I just wrote it as it happened. She took issue with it and sued me and sued the newspaper. That all amounted to nothing, but it was very stressful for a while. The Enterprise was totally behind me and stood up for me, and it got settled. It was the Sandwich Enterprise.

My sister was a reporter for The Landmark up in Princeton. The paper has just been taken over by Gatehouse Media. They've taken over the Cape Cod Times and the Worcester Telegram, and they bought out The Landmark. My sister got a buyout. That's the end after 30 years. That's what Gatehouse does. It's like the small hospitals have all been bought out by the big ones and small grocery stores. That's the trend. My sister will retire now. She's 75. She started up with them when I left. It used to be the Holden Landmark but with the change of ownership that went to just Landmark. Her name is Phyllis Booth.

BS: *I found an article titled, "Guard's latest base vision sees continued training." The first line reads: BARNSTABLE—Judy Koenig looked at the massive document in front of her and shook her head. "It's full of a lot of words but has very little to say," the Sandwich resident said.*

JK: In 1999, I was on the Community Working Group to develop a master plan for the Massachusetts Military Reservation. There were representatives from the state, county, and local representatives on that committee. It was a bit tense. The military was not very welcoming to outsiders asking questions, putting them on the spot. But over time, it all smoothed out — the base needed to be cleaned up. There was a lot of toxic stuff in the water that was leaching into the groundwater and affecting nearby towns. It was from all the unexploded ammunition that they used for training. It wasn't just people like me. We had the State, and the Senate involved. They were all on the same committee. There was a bit of good political pressure.

BS: *How, without cell phones and the technology from today, were you able to get stories?*

JK: A few would come from the editor, but most were from tips and leads from inside of government. I won't identify anybody yet. But I gained the trust of the people I was writing about. I would get leads on items that nobody knew about but needed to be looked into, and I would follow up on it. The people trusted me. That's why it worked. The other thing is I've had a police scanner ever since I started. And I still have it, and I still listen to it. There would be a bad accident or a near-drowning; something and I would just pick up the camera and go. That's where I got a whole lot of pictures and stories. Very satisfying. I'm glad I had a newspaper career.

BS: *Are your children nearby?*

JK: Just Jim, thank goodness. He's in the next town over, and the youngest is in Florida. My oldest son died in an accident.

BS: *Thank you for showing what a woman, a wife, a mother of three can do.*

JK: There's a lot of history to what it was like. It was meaningful. There's so much lack of meaning in many things these days.

## Judy Koenig—Part 2

About a week after Judy and I talked, she sent me an email writing, "I forgot to tell you that I covered three murders between 1981 and 1982 here in town. They were pretty gruesome. The village Broadsider at the time cost 20 cents!"

BS: *That was an intriguing email you sent me. So, who got murdered?*

JK: The first one was in June of 1985. It seems that an ex-girlfriend found out the old boyfriend was seeing somebody else. She went to his home, shot them both in the head, and set the house on fire. She wasn't happy. They got her, and it wasn't like they couldn't figure out who did it. They knew who it was. She had a history locally. They said they were "famil-iar with her." Reading from her article: "Investigated previous problems with this man and woman. The man that was killed and the ex-girlfriend and we have taken action against the woman in the past." I had that clip in my portfolio. I went the next morning. I took pictures and investigated asking questions of the police officers and the chief. They had already removed the bodies. I don't know what she got. They sent her to Taunton State Hospital for 20 days for observation.

That was that one and then in March of 1986, this middle-aged man from the town was at a local bar, and two younger guys were there, and they were all drinking beer. The story is that the older guy invited them back to his house to play pool and have some more beer. But behind the scenes, not reported was the fact that it was a homosexual event. I don't know what happened in the house, but the older man was killed. They did get both guys. They couldn't find the body for a while, and when they did, it was buried in a very abandoned area off Cape sort of in the woods. They found the body, the criminal's car, and other evidence.

BS: *How did they find the body?*

JK: It was just a lot of good police work. An oriental rug from the guy's home was stolen, and they saw traces of this and other things that were taken from the house. It was a camouflaged grave. Judy reads from the paper clipping, "that was covered with a large quantity of lime, and indi-cations were that Howard had received extreme head and neck wounds. Two trash bags full of bloody towels, other linens were found a short distance away along with a rug pad." They wrapped him up, put him in the trunk of their car, and off they went. It wasn't until relatives of his couldn't get a hold of this man, and they went to the house, went in, and could see something had happened there. There was a lot of blood splat-ter, broken pottery, and it looked like there had been a fight. It looked like attempts were made, Judy continues reading. "Several areas of the house there were cleaned up and removed the bloodstains."

BS: *How do you take that kind of situation? It's disturbing.*

JK: In fact, the first murder here was the first in town since 1968. So, almost twenty years. I was reading the report from when the people were in the house. It was not a very nice thing, wrapping him up and stuffing him in the trunk. He was 'innocently' inviting them back to the house, and he may have had something else in mind. It looked like they didn't like it.

BS: *I was listening back to your transcript, and it's an interesting life. You went from a nurse to an investigative reporter and a selectman. I'll put you up against any of the guys I've talked to. You said you lost one of your sons in an accident. May I ask how?*

JK: Steve was my oldest. He had a seizure disorder from an early injury, and he was doing okay, but we guessed that he hadn't picked up his prescription for medicine. He was 27 at the time and had a seizure at the wheel of the car and died instantly from the crash. It is sad, and it's something that you don't ever get out of your mind. Women have the strength of character, more than men.

## Chapter 8

---

## John Milne—Rolodex Connection:
## UPI Concord NH Bureau Manager

---

*John Kennedy, Edmund Muskie, Helen Thomas*

In 1960, John Milne talked his way into a John Kennedy press conference when JFK was running for president. Milne was fifteen. That led to an amazing fifty-year career reporting the news. Milne was on the desk when a news tip came in that there was an auto accident on Chappaquiddick. He talks about William Loeb and the infamous Union Leader letter to the editor, known as the Canuck letter. He was one of just three reporters covering Senator Edmund Muskie's speech in front of the Manchester Union Leader, and Muskie cried, or did he?

Sadly, John Milne passed away last year. His passing makes this recollection even more important.

**BS:** *Tell me about Newspaper Row.*

**JM:** Newspaper Row was Washington Street. It was a series of newspaper buildings. If you know that movie theater Pi Alley that's from the old Post, one of the old Boston papers, where they would throw unsorted type out and Pi was the measure. It's short for Pica. The Globe was there, and the Record was over in Winthrop Square, which was just behind it. The old Herald Traveler was there before they moved to the other side of Chinatown. I don't know the story, but there is a building up there that's called the United Press Building, and the legend I heard was one of the old UP guys, I think his name was Henry Minott, conned the landlord into setting the words United Press in the doorway. On election nights and big athletic days, we'd have these big signs, big display things on which they would hang votes. They had a little machine with a diagram, so for example for the World Series, they could diagram who was on base.

On big days, the street would be full of Bostonians trying to find the news. These are the days when you got extra editions every couple of hours.

The Record had a bulldog. A bulldog is a morning edition out on the streets shortly after sundown so that you could read in the evening. If you wanted to know what was the latest, for example, the Titanic sinking. These were the days when there was stiff competition among all these guys led by the rivalry between the United Press and Associated Press and the International News Service, which was owned by Hearst. UP and INS merged in the late '50s to form UPI.

BS: *Where were you?*

JM: When the UPI left newspaper row in the early to mid-'60s, I went to Ashburton Place. It's a little street that runs on the harbor side of Beacon Hill, that's Bowdoin Street where John Kennedy allegedly lived. This was back in the days of presidential hotels, and Kennedy had one on Bowdoin Street. Ashburton Place was around the corner. It's now a state office building.

BS: *Where are you from?*

JM: I was born in Indianapolis. My father was in the army, and we went to my mother's parents in Pittsburg, Kansas. We flew on a plane. My aunt and uncle were there, and somebody could help her deal with me. I have a sister who was born in 1950. She died in 1998. When my father got out of the army, we went to live with my other grandparents, who lived in Kansas City, Missouri, which was where I lived for my first five or six years of my life.

My grandfather came from Scotland and was illiterate. He was one of those guys they 'put on the boat.' My sister had a teapot that one of them, either my grandfather or grandmother, had on the boat that brought them over. The point was this was before Ellis Island, like 1875. My grandmother would never let him talk about it. She just thought it was outrageous that my great grandmother would put him on a boat and send him away. He stayed with a brother in Canada and then came to Kansas City. Kansas City was building a streetcar system, and it attracted people from all over for work. They were building a railroad.

My grandfather is one of those real stories, not one of those Horatio

Alger stories. He taught himself to read through the Masonic Ritual. The grammar is very clean. He became a Freemason, and you have to memorize a whole lot of stuff and part of the rituals. The point is he taught himself to read and write through that. He was one of those guys who could be happy reading the phone book. He rose to be the senior civil servant of the Kansas City streetcar system. He was badge number three, and the two above him were political appointees.

BS: *In your life, you are a long-time reporter. When did you devote yourself to journalism?*

JM: I have reported the news for fifty years. I had always been interested in reading newspapers and news. I got a merit badge from the Boy Scout for news. If you wanted to rise in the ranks, you had to get so many merit badges like camping and hiking, and one of them was news. I had to take this current affairs test. A friend of mine in high school and I were competitive all the way through. He was considered the school brain because he was very, very smart. We had moved several times from Kansas City to Omaha, where my father got a job. We moved within Omaha to a different school district, and I'm the fresh new sophomore. Steve is the venerable brain. We tied on a history test. It was a shock to everybody, even me, because there were questions of current affairs on the test, and I got them all right. I pretty well knew what I was going to do in 1964 during the Goldwater election.

I had become acquainted with the publisher and one of the editors of the Grinnell Herald Register. This was before the AP consortium counted ballots. You had to do it yourself. The Union Leader used to do it in New Hampshire. They had somebody in every clerk's office, and, as soon as the clerk was done, they would have reserved a phone in the town hall, and they'd call in the number of votes on the ballots. However, in 1964, in Iowa, they didn't do that. They needed a bunch of people to count ballots, and what was easier but getting a bunch of college kids. They asked me to round up some to help count ballots, and that was my first election night.

BS: *You have questioned every president in your life.*

JM: In 1960, when I was in high school, I talked my way into a press conference with John Kennedy. They didn't have security until November

22, 1963. I said I was writing stuff for my school paper, which wasn't true. They didn't care. They just wanted a room full of people. So, I asked some stupid questions. I don't remember a question, but it was probably about youth, something like, "Are you too young to do this?" Of which of course, he was ready for that.

BS: *Do you remember what he looked like, how he sounded?*

JM: I remember he sounded young because he had that Boston accent. When you're fifteen, everybody over thirty looks older. That was my first adventure in journalism.

BS: *I love that story. What are your years and dates with UPI? Where did you get started?*

JM: I had a friend in college whose father worked for UPI in Washington, DC. In the last half of my senior year, I went out there, and I met Grant Dillman, who ran the office. He was the bureau manager, and Grant took a shine to me, and he said, "Send your resume to all these people, and I'll send a letter." I did that, and I got a response from the UPI bureau in Raleigh, North Carolina. I got the job, which was a jack of all trades. In UPI, the distinction of the wire services between a reporter and an editor is much less clear than other places. You're going to run out to cover a news conference and then the next minute somebody's calling. It's a stringer who is calling in a story that you have to take down and organize their reporting in a publishable document. In a place like Washington, there were reporters and real editors and a rewrite man. In Raleigh, you had to do a little of everything. Dave Haskell was everything in the Boston bureau. He came in at five, and that was back when afternoon newspapers provided the bulk of revenue because there were so many of them. He would organize the whole daily report.

BS: *How do you learn everything?*

JM: One of the things they teach you is more by trial and error. They throw you into the pond to see if you can swim. Every paragraph you write in a big crashing, breaking news story, you hand that story to the operator who puts it on the wire. You have to be very careful about every word. It teaches you to think about every word more than if you were writing something down, and you had the opportunity to go back and check it.

BS: *It's like those who are posting items without research or with bias.*

JM: What I find is scary is people are willing to put out stuff before it is thoroughly checked out. My rule has always been that whatever happens in the first impression, a plane crash, a political crisis, a coup, the first report is always going to be wrong. There's going to be something wrong with it. It's the fog of war. It's the first person you talked to didn't really see it. Back in the day, you had a system where you had to be careful about that stuff. Today, with that attitude or need to be competitive at all hazards, you get it wrong. There are any number of stories that get it wrong because we are so polarized. People take advantage of what basically are human mistakes.

What I found more interesting is the Benghazi business. The critics of the state department admitted they had an agenda to make Mrs. Clinton look bad and seized on so many of these. "Oh well, first, it was a response to something that happened in Cairo." Well, no, it was a planned attack.

BS: *There was a report that the anti-Islam movie inflamed the situation.*

JM: Whoever first talked about it didn't know and said maybe it was that movie. Clinton's lying about the movie. Is the intent part of the definition of a lie?

Let me contrast that with a real fake news event. It was late some evening in Boston, and there were two of us, and probably a teletype operator. A message comes in from the UPI bureau in Hartford. They're sending in this little story that says there was a state police trooper who was moonlighting driving a Good Humor truck. He sees a traffic violation, pulls over the motorist, and gives him a ticket. I remember coming in, and Guy Darst was the senior guy in the bureau at that time, and I say, "You better look at this." He looks at it and calls the guy in Hartford. I only heard one side of the conversation,

"Bruno, this sounds like an old chestnut. Do you know what an old chestnut is? It's an old story that people keep repeating, but it isn't true." This goes on, and Durst says, "Will you go and check this out?" Bruno gets back on the phone a few minutes later, and in this meek little voice says there aren't any state troopers pulling over Good Humor trucks. That's the silliest thing. However, we had sent out a story on the wire. So, then we sent out a correction. Guy says, "I'll bet you that was some PIO, Press Information Officer, who's on some military base who's got to work all night, and he's bored, and he thought he'd cause some trouble." He calls in a fake news story.

You wouldn't believe the number of times that I got a call suggesting that Jimmy Cagney was dead. He lived in Edgartown, Massachusetts. Somebody didn't like him running his lawnmower or something, and they would call, and invariably, the New York Daily News would hear of it, and they would call UPI saying, "Hey, we got this report that Jimmy Cagney is dead. Can you write an obit?" This was right after Chappaquiddick, 1969. So, this is the middle of the night, and I call up Dominick Arena, who was the Edgartown police chief at the time. Go back to the Chappaquiddick clips. He's all over the place. He said, "I talked to him this morning. I would have known if he was dead."

To go back to the Connecticut fake news trooper story, some disc jockey that comes in that morning reads the first story over the air but doesn't read the correction. It's eight in the morning, and everyone is driving to work, and the DJ reads this story. Well, one of the people on his way to work hearing the story is the Connecticut Director of Public Safety. He throws a fit. He's got an investigative staff, which he assigns to find out where this story came from, which was, in fact, the PIO on the night shift at the New London Coast Guard. I think he was bored. He calls in the story. Maybe he had a bet with another guy saying I can get this on the wire. I don't know what it was, but he did make the call. So, we did kill the story belatedly. The Connecticut Director gets wind of it and investigates. He did not take a joke. He got on the phone with some politician he knew, and he wanted something done about this guy. The guy got sent to Vietnam.

BS: *The PIO guy got sent to Vietnam?*

JM: Yes. This is where the story festered until Jack Anderson, the syndicated columnist, found out about it. He writes a story that the Pentagon is leaning on this poor guy. Everybody is covered with mud except Guy Darst. I told that story at his funeral.

**BS:** *Do you go from Raleigh to Boston?*

**JM:** I got laid off in Raleigh. The bureau manager liked another guy better than he liked me, and the other guy could take photographs.

**BS:** *Where did you go after Raleigh?*

**JM:** I messed around and looked for a job, wasn't married. I went back to Washington to see Dillman. Somewhere along the line, I met HL Stevenson, who was the editor of the whole UPI service. He's a really interesting guy. He ran the UPI in the south during civil riots, and he was the guy who kept saying, "You got to be straight." Most of the southern papers were locked into the establishment. Many of the AP papers were blaming outside agitators. It was pretty ugly.

**BS:** *However, Stevenson's policy was, "you have to be straight."*

**JM:** He had grown up in Mississippi. He had said to some reporter who was getting a job, "What do you think about segregation?" The reporter said, "I haven't thought about it very much." Stevenson says, "Well, think about it." He is one of those untold heroes of American journalism. Without him, you wouldn't have Claude Sitton, a reporter, editor, and a Pulitzer Prize winner. You wouldn't have David Halberstam, who came out of Harvard Crimson. He went to work for the Nashville paper, which was one of the few papers who tried to play it straight.

**BS:** *What did Stevenson see in you?*

**JM:** I do not know. I met him when I was still in Raleigh. Stevenson's wife, I never knew her real name, but she went by Bunny, a southern bell from the next town over. I think it was Cary, North Carolina. He came into the bureau to check messages, and I met him. I don't know what he saw in me, but he did. When I was laid off, I went to Washington, and I made the round-robin again, and I ended up in Boston. I think one of those unmentioned deals where I was twenty-two and looked sixteen, and they needed people to cover campus unrest. I got to Boston right after the Harvard strike in 1969.

**BS:** *I'm not familiar with that, the Harvard Strike.*

JM: The students at Harvard protested all sorts of stuff, the war, racism. I was on the desk, and some tip comes in; there was an auto accident on Chappaquiddick. This was a Sunday or weekend. We're calling around and all of a sudden somebody finds out whose car it was. It was Kennedy's car. In the quaint vernacular, all hell broke loose. UPI sent a guy down there. I was on the other end of the phone through the whole mess. If you care, Steve Kurkjian of the Globe was an intern from Northeastern. The Globe got this tip, and they sent Kurkjian down. From that not necessarily modest beginning, Steve made a whole career with the Globe-winning at least two Pulitzer Prizes. He's the intern and, some editor says, "Get down there and see what you can find out." This is something that no longer happens."

BS: *Who calls you? Who calls the Boston bureau?*

JM: Either somebody at the Globe or the Herald or somebody at a radio station or from the Cape Cod Times, who was a client of UPI, calls and said there's been this accident on Martha's Vineyard. Everybody is working on the story. UPI had a source inside the courtroom when they had the inquest. And, to this day, I will limit it to that. We were getting direct quotes from the inquest.

BS: *Talk about the freelance photographers you used?*

JM: Allan Papkin was a photo editor and photographer at UPI in the Boston bureau. However, at the risk of a digression, Dave Wurzel was the New England photo manager who used to provide film to any number of freelance photographers. He got the first call on the negatives. There used to be this wonderful competition. There was a Howard Johnson's on Albany Street in Boston, and these guys all had police scanners in their cars. There would be a fire or shooting or something, and all of these cars would light out and go sailing off to wherever it was to take pictures. Dave was giving them a decal and a couple of rolls of film. He created enough of a relationship with them that they'd call it into him. It was Dave's way of making sure he didn't miss anything that was going on in Boston.

BS: *He provided the means. All they had to do was put it in the camera and shoot.*

**JM:** Among those, I think Allan Papkin was one of those guys. Another one was Doug Mills, who is now the White House photographer for the New York Times. Ask any photographer in New England about Dave Wurzel. 'Father Dave.' That's what we called him. He was a big guy who was losing the sharpness of his eyesight but did all the work. He didn't trust himself to take pictures as much as he used to. He'd be in his office with three different people at the same time speaking this fake Italian. He'd run off a bunch of Italian dishes as if he were speaking Italian. That was Dave. He was the UPI New England photo manager or some title like that.

**BS:** *So, Muskie never cried. You said, "I was being asked specifically did he cry, and I said no. And, then Dave Broder of the Washington Post said, Muskie, wept openly, which was Broder's lead. And then, that's why we all had to rush around and explain why we didn't have it." What happened? You were there.*

**JM:** My wife, Lisa, was there too. Lisa and I were supposed to go and cover a sled dog race in Laconia. But Muskie's going to give this speech in Manchester. The plan had been to swing by the thing and head for the sled dog race. This story became a big deal because Muskie had rented a flatbed and backed it up in front of the Union Leader when it was on Amherst Street. It was snowing and miserable in January. There were three of us who used the flatbed truck as an umbrella to take notes. It was me, Joe Zellner of the AP, and Richard Lee Strout. He was a reporter for the Christian Science Monitor, and he had this TRB column in The New Republic.

**BS:** *TRB?*

**JM:** TRB was a reversal of the Brooklyn Rapid Transit. That's how he got the copy to the magazine. We were the closest witnesses. We are holding our notebooks under the flatbed.

**BS:** *Okay, got it. It's miserable, snowing, wet. You're holding your paper notebooks under the flatbed to keep them dry.*

**JM:** Right. Muskie comes out. The issue was that the Union Leader published a letter to the editor signed by someone named Frank Morrison, who alleged that at some political deal in Florida, somebody asked a race question. It was 1972. Segregation and busing were all over. A staffer of

Muskie's, unidentified, was supposed to have said, "We don't have niggers, but we have Canucks." The Union Leader just went berserk against Muskie. Frontpage Loeb editorials.

And it is most likely that it was one of the Nixon dirty tricks. I'm saying it because I don't know or remember where they were from, either the Committee to Reelect the President or if they were working in the White House. One of Nixon's guys tells a television reporter in a rather tender moment that he had written the Canuck letter.

BS: *In a tender moment? I love it.*

JM: Would you like another euphemism?

BS: *No, I love it. Nixon's guy had written the comment.*

JM: No, the letter itself. The Canuck letter. If you go back through the Union Leader stuff, there was a photocopy of the letter. What happened after the letter? Muskie denies it. I think this is a pretty direct quote about Loeb, "He doesn't walk. He crawls." At some point, Muskie chokes up. He told me ten years later that he was angry. Remember, I covered politics. So, if you accept the proposition that the White House wrote it, Muskie had a reputation for having a sharp temper. There's a famous story of a poker game with a bunch of reporters there, not me. He loses a pot. He loses something. He just threw a fit, probably his fault.

BS: *Muskie is standing on a flatbed in front of the Union Leader on this cold day, and this letter is published that says one of his men has made a derogatory remark about Canadians, calling them Canucks?*

JM: The letter is hurting Muskie on the west side of Manchester. He brings Severn Beliveau, who was at that time a speaker of the Maine House of Representatives, among other dignitaries from Maine, to say this guy is not prejudiced. Also, there was another incident. Newsweek, in its little gossip column, publishes this snotty thing about Mrs. Muskie, from what I can remember was utterly harmless. However, the Union Leader put it on the editorial page, somehow suggesting that Mrs. Muskie was some kind of hoyden.

BS: *A hoyden? What's that?*

**JM:** A woman who is somewhere between loud and brash, and probably the implication was a kind of goofy woman. They gave her a couple of friends to campaign with her. Apparently, at the end of the day, she'd have a drink. When he gets to the point about his wife, it's when Muskie just gets furious, and then that's when he says this man doesn't walk; he crawls of Loeb. Remember, it's snowing like stink, and I'm watching. If he cries, if he says something, I've got to know.

**BS:** *He's bent over and holding himself. But he's not weeping.*

**JM:** As soon as he's through, I got to get a phone. I start running for a phone, and I see David Broder, and he's ashen. He's sort of shocked by all this. That's what got him to write about the tears rolling down his face or whatever it was.

**BS:** *"Wept openly. Tears streaming down his face" was the quote.*

**JM:** He called the Post, and the lead went on the LA Times, Washington Post news service wire. He's calling the office about the tears falling down his face. This lead goes on the Post wire. That's what leads are supposed to do. Then, everybody gets callbacks. The guy who called me back was the assistant manager named Bill Middlebrooks, like the third baseman. He says, "What's the story?" I said, "I was there, and he didn't cry." Middlebrooks says, "That's good enough for me." HL Stevenson asked me later about it. I said the same thing. "He didn't cry." And, he said, "That's good enough for me."

But the subsequent adventures of that story was that the Zellner story on AP gets topped with tears, somebody in New York or whatever writes a lead for Zellner's story with a Manchester dateline and a Zellner byline including the tears.

**BS:** *Let me get this straight. Someone from AP took Zellner's story and added the information to it that Muskie cried based on what they had heard, not what Zellner reported. Is that correct?*

**JM:** My dim memory about this is they never called him. It was competitive journalism. Broder subsequently told me, and I think it's in one of his memoirs, that he went over the top, that he had gone too far in the description. There's also a Wall Street Journal story by Jim Parry, a great reporter, who writes one of those Wall Street Journal stories several days later that basically said I was an idiot because I didn't see these tears for what it was.

BS: *What was it like to work on a wire service?*

JM: Wire service work was remarkably intense because you were outnumbered and outgunned every time and everywhere you looked by the competition. You had to win by skill and chutzpah. We competed with AP, the other papers, and the networks.

BS: *I found this article that you wrote, "Thursday, May 1, 1975, End of Vietnam War. No fanfare, no celebration, no nothing," by John Milne. Washington. It's a great article. What Kissinger is saying is nothing, you say.*

JM: I've been lied to by all of them, including Kissinger. The definition of reporting in Washington, which I think I stole from somebody, is you stand around in front of a closed-door waiting for some politician to come out and lie to you.

BS: *The Great Finnigan Sandbag, "the Union Leader editorialist, charged that Milne's story was a blatant editorial attempt to link this visit by the governor to the so-called tax surge controversy here in New Hampshire." And, you said, "Milne insisted he was confident his story was as accurate as I could make it." This was an article in the Union Leader from 1973.*

JM: I hesitate to go too far down this road, but those of us who covered Meldrim Thomson, Jr. know what it's like to cover Donald J. Trump. Thomson was smarter than Trump. I'm saying that objectively. Thomson was brilliant, and I don't know who found who, but he linked up with Loeb. Thomson had been a school board member or something like that in Orford, New Hampshire. He had a law book publishing company that was up there. However, at the school board, he refused to take federal funds and made a big scene out of it. I didn't know whether, and this is where I don't know whether he found Loeb or Loeb found him. Here is this crusader for anti-federal funds. He's right out of one of those Southern politics guys like WJ Cash, and basically what he figured out was in those southern primaries winning the primary is tantamount for winning the election. There is no issue because the only issue is segregation, and they were all for it. So, how do you set yourself apart from the pack? Usually, it's by being more outrageous than the next guy. You have Earl Long, you have Herman Talmadge, and you have a couple of those guys in Florida that were just outrageous personalities. Thomson gets up to New Hampshire, and he finds it's the mirror image of the Southern pattern. They're all Republican. They only issue is, are you against taxes enough?

If you wanted to get attention or you wanted to win a primary in New Hampshire, he figured out you had to have a way to get attention. Thomson was very good at that, and Loeb backed him up.

With Loeb, you had to do a little criminology with this. I won't bore you with my comparison theory of how closely the Union Leader matches Pravda. But it's true. Like Pravda, whoever the Union Leader called to get a quote on some issue, you knew Loeb's moving him up. When the deputy commissar of agricultural production stands up there in the Red Square to watch the troops walk by, that's a signal that the old deputy commissar is on his way up.

BS: *Right. You don't get invited to that party and not be somebody. What did Thomson do?*

JM: What this led to was in January, Thomson's first month in office, it's snowing like mad. It's snowing so badly that the state sends everybody home. That's bad. Thomson freaks out. He sends Fred Goode, who was his chief of staff who is now a retired judge, over to the DRA, the Department of Revenue Administration tax office, and he wants to see specific taxpayer's returns. Those included his political enemies.

BS: *Wow. Specific taxpayers. Did he want to see their returns?*

JM: Yes. Specific taxpayer returns. Remember, in those days, the New Hampshire tax return got the first page of the federal tax return. There are two casts of characters in this story. I think he asked for Tom McIntyre's return, the sitting senator who was a democrat, Stuart Lamprey's, and president of the senate who worked for Walter Peterson. Even with this terrible weather, there had to be somebody there at the office.

BS: *So, he got them?*

JM: He got to look at them. But, sooner or later, somebody wakes up and says you got to have a little more authorization than I want to see a tax return. Charles G. Douglas III, later a congressman and then a Supreme Court judge, goes over to the New Hampshire Hospital with a request for the files of specifically identified people.

BS: *Do they go to the New Hampshire Hospital for medical files?*

JM: Psychiatric files. Thomson, himself, gets in a car with Dick Flynn, then the commissioner of safety, and they drive to Wellesley, Massachusetts. In 1968, the Safe Streets Act passed, which was the first weak gun control stuff. They banned Saturday night specials and mail-ordered sales of stuff. One of the things this also did, because this was 1968, was they banned police agencies from keeping files without probable cause - a perfectly constitutional thing to do. What happened, in reality, was all of those files were sent to public/private operations, and there was one in Wellesley called the New England Organized Crime Information System or something like that. And Thomson does the same thing.

BS: *What files is he looking for?*

JM: These are organized crime files, but they're also raw crap that's been saved by police agencies. They got collected in this outfit by the police agencies but couldn't keep them because of the law. The police are banned from keeping them in their departments. The police argued, with some justification, that they needed organized crime files. There were also things on radicals. Access to these files was restricted only to the Attorneys General of the five states. Connecticut has a different system where the attorney general of Connecticut is a civil lawyer, and the state's attorneys of the counties are the chief prosecuting officers and the head of the state police. They are the only ones who are supposed to access these files.

Thomson goes down there with Flynn, commissioner of safety. He's not supposed to access the files, but arguably, he would do it. Thomson wants somebody with a badge to walk in there with him. He starts asking for specific names. This one gets a little funnier because one of them is

Wesley Powell, a regular candidate for something. Warren Pease is requested. He owns a printing office in the Upper River Valley that arguably would have competed with Thomson's law book printing shop, and that may have been the one that had McIntyre, the Democratic senator, in it. But these were a lot of specific names who would have presumably not had much contact with organized crime.

**BS:** *Were these people in the organized crime files?*

**JM:** He asked for the names. All he got, before somebody woke up to this in Wellesley, was that he might have gotten to know whether there was a file in existence, which would have been a significant piece of data. There was a lot of rumor and unfounded stuff about Boston gangsters using New Hampshire as a dumping ground for money laundering and all sorts of stuff.

**BS:** *Did he get a name?*

**JM:** We don't know. He got thrown out. We do know he went down there, and he may have gotten information that suggested there was a file. These were his political and commercial rivals and people like Wes, who might have posed a threat. Who knows why Warren was in there.

That hits the news. I wrote the Wellesley one, and Rod Paul from the Monitor wrote the tax search one, and I don't know if anyone has ever written the New Hampshire Hospital one. That's the context for this. This was a big story - abuse of power. The legislature is investigating, and every other newspaper is just going through gallons of ink going through this. This is why I made the comparison.

The Union Leader the next morning says that Thomson was investigating security at all of these places, and I was the one at fault for writing about it. Mel was doing his job. They started an investigation. Although, he did have the state police follow us. That's the context. Chris Spiro, who had a job teaching at the community college or someplace, was there to talk about objectivity in news gathering or something like that. Finnegan shows up and reads his editorial talking about what a jerk I am.

**BS:** *Finnegan?*

**JM:** James Finnegan was an editorial writer for the Manchester Union

Leader. You got to remember there is a UPI piece of this. Loeb was married to Nackey Scripps, who had one-fifth of my little pop stand. It required a certain amount of tightrope walking to do that. When I got interviewed by the Watergate prosecutor, Loeb wrote a letter to some boss or another saying, "That's because he's an activist. He's trying to blow the whistle," which was untrue. This is the closest set of political adventures to the modern-day that I can imagine. There isn't any Fox News, but they had the Union Leader who wanted to be a player in the political universe.

BS: *The Union Leader was then as Fox News is now to politics?*

JM: The Union Leader was considered an influential voice among conservatives. Now it's significantly less so. I don't know if Joe wants to put out a real newspaper or be a kingmaker. There are times when he will get going. He will really go at it, and the next day he'll get off on something else. However, that's how I got into the Union Leader for that particular article.

BS: *Would you speak about Helen Thomas?*

JM: I was privileged to work with her, and I always say, I was privileged to carry her briefcase, metaphorically. Helen was one of those people who was unafraid, unlike many of her Washington colleagues, to ask a simple direct question that went to the heart of an issue. Part of the Washington game was always not to offend the press secretary you're having lunch with. There was always this back and forth, but Helen asked the question that the little old lady in the laundromat would ask if she was there. She worked on it. I, on occasion, helped her do the first question, which is always granted to the wire services.

BS: *The wire services sit in the front row for the press briefings.*

JM: Yes. And, if you do it right, which is what Helen always tried to do, it sets the tone for the press conference. So, if you ask a question about the deficit, then there will be some secondary follow up. The president gets to do this because he has a chart of all the names in front of him, and if it's getting a little hot, he'll say, "Oh Sarah McClendon. Sarah, what's your question?" Sarah was one of those Washington characters who would have this long preface that nobody could understand. She had a bunch of little newspapers in Texas. And so it was an important question for 20,000 people down in Texas, but nobody was going to brief the president on this thing. So, she has to go on and on to the point that one time, President Eisenhower said, "Mrs. McClendon, are you asking a question or making a speech?" It is tactically important for the president to be able to get people off the subject he doesn't want to talk about. One of Helen's most important contributions was to ask that question that the president didn't want to talk about. I loved her. At a party for Helen, I introduced her, and I said you remember Lisa, and without blinking, Helen said, "Where's my lemon cake?" Lisa would bake a lemon cake for some reason, and we did some socializing with her and Doug.

**BS:** *Doug Cornell was her husband.*

**JM:** It was one of the great love stories of all time. Doug was the AP reporter, and she worked for UPI. When UPI was owned by the Moonie organization, she walked out. To many people, she was UPI. She and Doug became close. Doug Cornell of the AP may have been and probably was the greatest wire reporter I ever met. The great story of Doug's was that he was writing the main lead for a convention, I believe it was in Philadelphia 1948, and everything broke down. AP used to file with Western Union and the Western Union system was out. So, Doug walked over to a telephone, picks it up, and Doug dictates the convention main lead off the top of his head and out of his notebook. It's an accomplishment. This was back when the political conventions actually chose the presidential candidates. He and Helen were pals because they were old together, and finally, when Doug retired, they got married. Nancy Reagan broke the news. He was probably 65, and she was mid-fifties. They had phones on each bedside table in case the office called.

**BS:** *A real love story. Can you tell me a story about the Rolodex?*

**JM:** When I used it, there was a card on one of the Vanzetti's, Sacco & Vanzetti. It was a cousin or sister or somebody. Old Hank Minott actually obtained Vanzetti's last letter in which he proclaimed, going to the chair, proclaimed his innocence. That's back when there were real scoops.

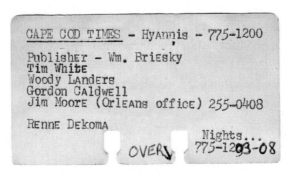

*Chapter 9*

---

## Sherwood Landers: Rolodex Connection: Card on File

---

*Cape Cod Times, Living with Multiple Sclerosis*

In "My Cousin Vinny," Marisa Tomei is on the witness stand acting as an automotive expert under oath and giving testimony. She makes this understood by saying that her father is a mechanic. Her uncle is a mechanic. Her brother is a mechanic. She's worked on cars as well. Sherwood "Woody" Landers is a newspaper expert. Although he would be hard-pressed to want or use that label. Woody's father was a newspaperman. His brother was a newspaperman, and he is a newspaperman. The trio started a chain of newspapers in New York State and ran those weeklies for many years.

Woody Landers worked for the Cape Cod Times, a client of UPI, for 32 years, all the while dealing with the effects of multiple sclerosis. In his first week at the newspaper, the Chappaquiddick drowning story broke. Senator Ted Kennedy drove off a bridge on the tiny Massachusetts island and Mary Jo Kopechne died. He was a reporter, editor, and photographer. The lowest time of this gentle man's life was kissing his beloved wife of 56 years goodnight, and the next morning, she didn't wake up.

BS: *Let's start with your history. What newspaper did you begin with?*

SL: When I was 18 or 19, I went to Community College. My brother came home from Korea, and my father, my brother, and I began a small chain of weekly newspapers in Hyde Park, Dutchess County, New York. We ran the weeklies for many years. I sort of got tired of that, and I went to the Cape and applied for a job at the Cape Cod Times. It was 1969. I got a job as the assistant Sunday editor, and through the years, I became a news editor and a regional editor. Eventually, I was managing editor at one time. Reporting was my thing, and newspapers were my life. I still read the paper every day from cover to cover because I'm interested in the news. Ten or twelve years ago, I retired after 32 years at the Cape Cod Times. For the last fifteen years, I was a staff photographer, which I did until the end.

BS: *You said at one time that between you, your father, and your brother, you had 100 years of newspapering between you three.*

SL: My father started in Worcester, Massachusetts as a reporter at the Worcester Gazette. My brother came home from Korea, and he started with our papers. Hyde Park was the central place for producing our ten weekly papers. But he went off to Gannett and oversaw the production of newspapers. He went out to newspapers that needed help. He helped them organize the papers and the newsroom and did that for many years helping to develop the news and to process the news. He got things done because he was sort of a taskmaster. He was in Navy Intelligence, and maybe that affected his thinking ability to get newspapers to do what they had to do to satisfy the public.

In Hyde Park, I worked under two people, one was an AP photographer, and one was a UPI photographer. I trained under them for a time. George Brown was a stringer for UPI.

BS: *Tell me about the Cape Cod Times and some of the stories.*

SL: The week I came to the Cape Cod Times was the week of Chappaquiddick. I was a Sunday staffer in the newsroom. I had friends who had a radio station in New York. I made phone calls to them, keeping them updated on the Chappaquiddick thing. I called this radio station in Poughkeepsie three or four times to keep them updated too. I don't know if I violated anything, but it was an exciting time. I received phone calls from all over the world from people wanting information on Chappaquiddick. The phone was hot.

BS: *It was a great first week in regards to newspaper reporting.*

SL: I was with my family-owned weekly papers, so going to a daily paper was an exciting thing for me. I had to learn all over again what the news was about. I was writing feature stories, and my Sunday editor and I were the only staffers on the Sunday paper. We wrote everything. We photographed everything. We laid out pages for the Sunday paper. Bill Smith was the Sunday editor, and I was the assistant. You had to be everything, reporter, editor, photographer, to do the job of assistant Sunday editor. That's where I gained most of my skills by spending time with Bill Smith, who was an excellent writer, photographer, and reporter. We were good friends. He's deceased now, but we had a great time producing Sunday papers.

BS: *When you were there, William Briesky was the publisher?*

SL: William Briesky was at a paper in New Hampshire, the Fosters Daily Democrat, and then he came to the Cape Cod Times as editor. I worked for Bill, who was a great editor, very driven, and very upfront. He was good to work for. Very demanding, but very concentrated on doing a great job every day. Tim White was an assistant Sunday editor. He was sharp, and he worked on the daily side of the copy desk. Everyone had a turn on the copy desk as far as their growth. It's a good testing ground for those who want to stay in newspapers and prove themselves.

BS: *Who was Gordon Caldwell?*

SL: Gordon Caldwell was one of two photographers. He and Louis Laprade were both staff photographers. They were the daily side, and I was the Sunday side. Lou had a lot of pictures from Chappaquiddick. One was taken at the Barnstable Airport of Teddy Kennedy with a neck brace on. He got to Teddy at the airport, and that photo wound up on the cover of Time Magazine. He had an exclusive picture. He and Gordon were both gentlemen.

BS: *I have it as the Cape Cod Standard-Times.*

SL: It was the Cape Cod Standard-Times. After several years, our publisher wanted to have a Cape Cod identity. So, he changed the name from the Standard-Times to Cape Cod Times. At the time, we had a New Bedford paper called the New Bedford Standard-Times. There was an overlap, but after they changed the name, we were running free and had our own identity. That's the way the publisher wanted it. The paper is an award-winning newspaper.

BS: *You photographed Nancy Kerrigan in 1994 before the Olympics.*

SL: Yes, at the Tony Kent Arena. I took her picture at the Tony Kent Arena, where she was practicing with her coach for the Olympics. I was assigned by the sports department to photograph her in South Dennis.

BS: *I have a photograph of yours that you took of the photographers who are waiting to photograph Nancy. You have the photo credit.*

SL: I got an outside shot of the photographers waiting for her to show up. It was a waiting game.

BS: *Another picture is a joyous Ted Kennedy conducting The Pops in 1997.*

SL: Pops on the Green, every year it comes to Cape Cod, and there's a guest conductor. He was the guest that year, and his family was in the audience. I photographed him many times.

BS: *I have a picture you took of Harold Russell, who was in the movie, "The Best Years of Our Lives." He had both his hands amputated after an accidental explosion.*

SL: I photographed him for a feature story. He won two Oscars.

BS: *Are you still doing the Polar Bear Plunge?*

SL: I used to do it until this year. I've done it probably eight or nine times. You see, I have MS, multiple sclerosis. The last time I went in was by using a walker. MS Magazine asked for pictures of me, and the picture ran of me being helped out of the water by two marines at Smuggler's Beach. That was a major thing for me. It's quite an experience.

You know why I did it? I did it because there are people who have MS that would want to do that but can't. I did it for those people who knew in their hearts they couldn't do it. You see, I have a support group for MS. We talk about MS and how it affects the body. I do this as an example of, if you want to do something, you do it regardless of what someone tells you. I pushed myself to do it. This year it was ten degrees. I chickened out.

BS: *What's it feel like to get in that frigid water?*

SL: I didn't feel much until the water got up over my knees. Once you get in, you dunk, and then you come out. I enjoyed doing it and met a lot of people. People were cheering me, and I said, don't cheer me. I'm not to be cheered. I just want to make those people with MS happier with what I did today.

BS: *Tell me about MS. When did you get it? What does it feel like?*

SL: The first bout with MS was probably 30 years ago when I got what they call ancient blindness, optic neuritis. They didn't have MRI's in those days. Now they do. I lost vision in my right eye. That was the first indication of MS. I still have that problem. It has the peripheral vision but not dead ahead vision. It's an interesting disease. You know depression is almost as bad as the physical part of it. You suffer from depression because your body is letting you down, and it's hard to react to it. It's one of those diseases that are unkind. I fight it every day, but I still work and drive. I'm lucky and blessed. I drive to Stop and Shop three days a week.

BS: *You first noticed it thirty years ago.*

SL: It was officially diagnosed ten years ago by a neurologist in Hyannis. I have the slow-moving version of MS. It will get progressively worse, but slowly. I still use a walker, and I still drive. It's painful sometimes, but I overlook a lot of things. I'm blessed. I'm trying to be sensitive to other people who can't do what I do. I go to a support group, where a man is being fed by his wife, while he sits in a wheelchair. I'm walking, and I'm talking, and I get in my car, and I drive away. Other people can't do it.

BS: *Do you work at Stop and Shop?*

SL: I work at Stop and Shop three days a week. I was there for twelve years and left because of my illness, my MS. I thought maybe I would find the magic bullet to cure me, but physical therapy can only go so far. The manager, after I retired, hired me back under 'reasonable accommodation,' which is a kind of thing they do. He found a job I can do while I'm seated. I do promotions and fundraising like for children with cancer at Dana Farber. I do promotions on certain foods. The manager was very happy with my performance. I have a good time and meet a lot of great people, but I'm seated, and about the only person at Stop and Shop who does their job seated. This man, Paul Dupuis, created this job for me. He's a manager at another store now, but he created my job, and I do thank him for what he did for me.

BS: *That's great what he did for you. How old are you, Woody?*

SL: I'll be 79 tomorrow. July 11 is my birthday.

BS: *Can I ask you about Linda? Do you mind talking about her?*

SL: My wife was diabetic. She was 74 years old. One night at the end of February, I said goodnight to her, and the next morning, she didn't wake up. She was in a hospital for two weeks on a breathing tube. At the end of two weeks, we decided to try her without the tube. She lasted a few hours, and she died. They had to take her off the tube because they couldn't leave her on the tube for longer than two weeks.

BS: *Was it your decision to take her off the breathing tube?*

SL: No, they had to. They couldn't leave her on it for more than two weeks. If she lived on a tube, she'd have to go someplace that would take her breathing on the tube. No place on the Cape could take her. Maybe another hospital. Then she wouldn't know who we were, what she was doing there for the rest of her life. The quality of life was gone. My daughters and I talked, and we said we have to do what's best for her. We were glad we did it. If there's no quality of life, why bother? It's tough to wind up in a hospital, the rest of your life unable to converse with anyone. Linda liked to talk and talked to people all the time. She was a member of Hadassah and an avid player of Mahjong, which she played every day. She liked to do these things, but after that, she couldn't. She couldn't do anything. And for her, there was no life. It was a terrible thing. Everyone came to her funeral at the synagogue.

BS: *I have that Linda had a lifelong love of books.*

SL: She was a school librarian and an art teacher for many years. Then, she came to the Cape, and she taught art. She retired when our two daughters were born. Eventually, she went back to work and became a librarian in the school. She did that for twenty-three years. Then, she retired and read all day long. She read, read, read. She knew her books, and she knew her children's books. She loved reading to children. This was one of her favorite things at school.

BS: *I think it's appropriate for you and me today that this is for a book.*

SL: About her, you could write a book. There's so much to say I couldn't get it into one day. She was a wonderful wife of 56 years. She was a wonderful person, driven, and kept me in line. I need someone to keep me in line.

BS: *Her obituary ends with, "Please wear her favorite color, purple."*

SL: Her sorority was Zeta Phi, and their color was purple. She loved purple, purple clothes, purple dishes; you name it. She was a purple lady. My daughter wrote in the obit, "Please wear purple." And the people at the funeral wore purple. The rabbi wore a purple tie and shirt for the ceremony. He's an amazing rabbi at the Cape Cod Synagogue. Everybody wore purple, and it was a joyous occasion for her, and me. I loved that the people remembered this was an important issue for my wife. That would have meant a lot to her.

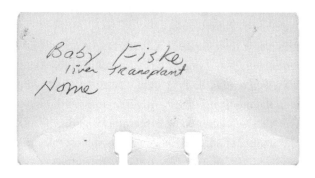

*Chapter 10*

---

Charlie Fiske: Rolodex Connection: Card on File

---

*Father of Baby Fiske, Liver Transplant and How to Save a Dying Child*

What does a father do when your seven-month-old baby daughter is dying and can only be saved with a liver transplant? The problem is that it's 1982, and there is no such thing as a transplant database to find one. How do you find a matching liver?

Jamie Fiske was born on Thanksgiving Day, 1981. A month later, her eyes were jaundiced. At two months, doctors operated on her, and that resulted in her looking healthier than before. However, a second operation was needed and done in July 1982. Her liver was failing.

After the operation, their doctor had a very candid question for Charlie revealing his long-term diagnosis for the little girl. The doctor asked, "Have you thought about having more kids?" It was a straightforward question.

With just four people working on the effort, time was of the essence. The Fiske family had one and a half months to get Jamie a new liver, or she would die. So, Charlie got publicity with the media and courted political types to get the story out to the public.

One tactic was to call Nancy Reagan, wife of President Ronald Reagan, every day for a month and a half. They called Ted Kennedy's office every day for a month and a half. They called Mike Barnicle, Boston Globe columnist, as well. "How many days does she have to live," is what he wanted to know. Charlie said that news people look for angles. They want to get the crux of the story. "Mike Barnicle stirred the pot." Charlie said, "He helped me get to the American people."

The family knew they needed publicity, but he noted, "You can't uninvite the media." He chose never to be critical of the media even when articles sometimes were less than accurate. Charlie believes, "Relationships are instant to the media types. It's critical to develop these relationships."

The American Academy of Pediatrics, an organization that is "dedicated to the health of all children," was having an annual conference in San Francisco. Charlie wanted to speak in front of the organization. They denied him the opportunity saying that only physicians could speak. Eventually, the AAP relented due to the unrelenting pressure that Charlie and his family used to convince the press and politicians to allow him to talk so that they could appeal for a liver for his daughter.

Determination and publicity saved Jamie Fiske. A family in Alpine, Utah, heard the speech. Five days later, in a tragic train/car crash, their son, Jess, was severely injured and dying. They donated the liver to Jamie.

It is hard to imagine a time when there wasn't a national list. Al Gore, congressman of Tennessee, called Charlie and said he wanted to do something about it. The White House called Charlie. He went to Washington, DC, and met with President and Mrs. Reagan. All the telephone calls had paid off. Ted Kennedy called and asked to help with a bill to establish a national database. In 1984, the US Congress passed the National Transplant Act. OrganDonor(dot)gov states, "The act established the Organ Procurement and Transplantation Network (OPTN) to maintain a national registry for organ matching."

Charlie notes, "Journalists taught him how to work with the media." Moreover, through it all, "We met a kind and caring general public who were supportive of us." He added, "We saw the best side of America."

Blue Cross and Blue Shield wrote a letter stating they would cover the transplant costs and naming "Kamie" Fiske. They got the name wrong. The hospital had a 'no conversation' conversation with the Fiske's. The

Minnesota hospital would pay if, for some reason, Blue Cross didn't. Massachusetts Governor Ed King said the State of Massachusetts would, "Pay a portion of the hospital bill." Jamie is alive and well today. Her father says, "She might be the longest living liver transplant survivor in the world."

At 68, Charlie is still an active proponent of health and service. Before joining the Arc of Massachusetts, whose mission is "to enhance the lives of people with intellectual and developmental disabilities, including autism, and their families," he spent two years in the Peace Corps serving in Malawi. Malawi is an African country and is listed by the United Nations as one of the 'least developed.' He said the two years there "provided a quiet environment for viewing how we live here in America."

---

## Chapter 11

## Don Davis—Rolodex Connection:
## Boston Bureau Manager

---

*Martin Luther King, Jr, and Gov. George Wallace, Vietnam Correspondent, New York Times Bestselling Author*

Don Davis was a journalist during the civil rights struggle, covering Dr. Martin Luther King, Jr, a Vietnam War photographer, a White House correspondent when Ronald Reagan was president, and a New York Times bestselling author for both fiction and nonfiction that included a book with astronaut Gene Cernan, the last man to walk on the moon and *Shooter: The Autobiography of the Top-Ranked Marine Sniper.* His work epitomizes what it means to have a hyphenated career. Davis spoke to me from his home in Colorado. His voice still has a sweet southern drawl from his home state of Georgia. He's funny, insightful, and modest.

*Note: It is with great sadness that I learned of Don's passing. I am so grateful for his time, his humor, and his devotion to the truth. Lucky me to have gotten to know him.*

BS: *You have quite a career. Thank you for talking with me today.*

DD: I'm just an old man laying around on a Sunday afternoon happy to have a little company.

BS: *I like to start at the beginning, your early life. You were born in Georgia in 1939, one of the greatest years in movie history; Gone With the Wind, Wizard of Oz, Stagecoach.*

DD: I was a little young to go to the movies at that time. But I was very lucky. The war came along, and some of my first memories are the blackouts we had. They'd turn off all the lights in the city, and I thought there was going to be an air raid that bad guys with planes were going to come to get us. But actually, the lights were turned off to not give a silhouette to German submarines passing off the coast. I was such a young kid at the time I really didn't understand. I had a great upbringing. My grandfather drove horse-drawn trolley cars on rails. He would let me ride with him and hold the reins sometimes. I thought that was a great experience.

BS: *Your father's name was Oden?*

DD: My father's name was Oden, and my mother's name was Artice. They named my sister Irma, so I was lucky to get out with a Don.

BS: *Where does Oden come from?*

DD: Nobody knew. It just was. They were country folks, and we were semi-rural during the depression. It was a tough time. The area we came from had a lot of foreign influences.

BS: *What did your dad and mom do? Did they work?*

DD: They tried different things. Remember, this was at the end of the depression, and they kept going bankrupt. He finally got a job with the Union Bag Paper Corporation. That was the steady paycheck he needed and insurance. He stayed for forty years. My mom sold real estate for a while but was primarily a homemaker. They had two children, me, and my sister Irma. We lived right next door to my grandmother and grandfather. They built their own houses. It was a good slow country kind of living for an adventurous young guy. I remember mom sometimes carried a revolver whenever she was hanging out clothes in case she needed to shoot rattlesnakes. We had these green walls of kudzu vines. It was just so much adventure there for any imagination. We didn't know we were poor. They took care of us and encouraged me. I remember the bookmobile coming by. It was like a truck that had been converted by the local library to take books out to folks who didn't have access to them. I used to raid that every time it came by. We had animals, pigs, horses, the usual stuff.

BS: *Country stuff.*

DD: Yea. The area that we lived in was heading out toward a tiny island. We had access to the ocean, which became very important in my later years when I got tired of playing in the kudzu and with the horses, and I discovered girls.

**BS:** *Beaches and bikinis do you mean?*

**DD:** There weren't bikinis back in those days, but the girls looked different than the guys. That was interesting to me.

**BS:** *Then you went to college?*

**DD:** First of all, I went to a community college called Armstrong College. My sister, who was the smart one in the family, had gone there, and I followed. We couldn't simply afford four years of tuition, and I had been accepted at the Citadel. I was going to go to the Army. I got a letter about six weeks before I was to report saying that because I had asthma while I was fourteen, and got an illness when I was very young, some typhoid fever thing that nearly killed me. They said that I could still come, but they couldn't guarantee me a commission. I wasn't going to go for four years and end up with no bars on my shoulders. It turned out to be a good thing because, by the time I was out of college, Vietnam was beginning to ramp up, and I would have been picked for sure. When I went to Armstrong, I made the mistake of wandering into the school newspaper office, and I was immediately smitten.

**BS:** *That's where you caught the germ of it?*

**DD:** I loved everything about it. From that point on, I went to school because I had to, and I started learning about newspapering. I hung around the Savannah Morning News and eventually worked for them. I got to know some of the guys. Television was just coming on.

I was the manager of the college radio station, and editor of the newspaper, and was getting my feet wet into the news business. Of all things, I graduated with a degree in mathematics. Strange. I still can't balance a checkbook. The reason for that was my family still remembered the depression and getting a steady job as an engineer was the ideal. Never risk your paycheck; you have family and responsibilities. I was tempted to call it a day right after I graduated because the space program was beginning. It was in its infancy. I remember one class in some geometry that when you finished the final exam, recruiters were waiting in the hallway with companies like Lockheed, and they were offering money on the spot to come to work down at the Cape. A lot of guys took it, and I said no, that was not what I wanted to do.

BS: *What year was that when you graduated?*

DD: My years are all off. I graduated in 1957, and that would have been about 1960, I guess. I didn't want to sit around in some drafting room, drawing straight lines. Now I had to find out what I would do because engineering was clearly out of my reach. I was never going to get into Georgia Tech or Auburn and didn't want to. I took some tests that showed that I should be a cop or a reporter. I didn't want to be a cop. We got too many of those in the family already, because of our Irish lineage. We had several people who carried badges. So, I went to Georgia, and that's where I fell into the mess because I quite frankly found that classroom work was boring. They had a great school newspaper that I joined. Down the street was the Athens Banner-Herald, which was the local newspaper, where I got a job to help pay for my tuition. I was the only reporter they had, and so I was learning the difference between classroom theory and life on the street. That was the one I loved the most.

BS: *Were you the only reporter they had? A college kid walks in off the street and gets hired.*

DD: We had a city editor, managing editor, and society editor. I would start my day off by going to the police court before going to class. It was a strange experience. I did everything. I helped layout the pages, and it was back in the days of Linotype. You could smell the ink, and I just loved it. That's where I learned to read type upside down and backward on the lead turtles.

BS: *I know about turtles. (Semi-circle forms that are used in the printing process).*

DD: It's hard to explain to somebody about turtles.

BS: *You're right, I've tried.*

DD: I was also in the Air National Guard at that time. All the guys had military obligations back then. And, luckily again, this was right before Vietnam. I didn't get involved with that, but we did get called to active duty three times, including the Cuban Missile Crisis. I was working at the Banner-Herald that summer, and I made a deal with the one professor I really liked, Charles Kopp. He had been a combat correspondent in World War II. We clicked. Unfortunately, he was teaching a class I didn't like. I think it was ethics. I'm working two jobs on the side, and just growing up. He took me aside after my first year at Georgia, my junior year, and he gave me a D in ethics. I said, "Hey, what's going on? I know I did lousy work and never did my homework." He looked me in the eye and said, "You're the one person in this class who is going to need this course. Retake it during the summer, and I guarantee you a B, but this time, pay attention." I said. "Okay, you got a deal." I was going to be working at the Banner-Herald all summer, and it turns out that somewhere in the middle of our deal, I got called to active duty and had to go defeat the Russians in Cuba. I'm convinced that Kennedy and Khrushchev finally settled because they knew I was on a truck ready. It was a scary time.

BS: *You didn't go to Cuba?*

DD: No, no, we just hung around the armory with the trucks loaded and ready to go. We were in Savannah, and Cuba was right down the coast. We fully expected Florida to be pretty much radioactive by that time. I was an airman second class, which is the lowest of the low. It was an obligation I had to do, but it was doing that or join the army.

BS: *Did you go to Georgia University?*

DD: The University of Georgia. Georgia Bulldogs.

BS: *We're on to Savannah Morning News.*

DD: Yep. I got a job with the Savannah Morning News on graduation. That didn't work out, luckily. I got fired from the Morning News. I was crossways with my city editor, and I got fired the same week that I got hired by Atlanta UPI. Instead of feeling bad, I celebrated and went to Atlanta. It was like I belonged there. I looked at those guys, and I said to myself, I can't do this. I just got fired from a little newspaper. I can't be what these guys are.

We had civil rights blowing up, and the Southern Division of UPI, back in the 1960s, was the best. We turned out geniuses covering all that crap. They were beautiful writers, great editors, great teachers, and they let me do it. I joined the team doing the little scutwork first, and next thing I know, I'm transferred over to Montgomery, Alabama. That put me right into the teeth of it. Instead of being bored with writing wedding notices and court proceedings, I'm carrying a pistol in clam country as I'm traveling back roads at night in Alabama, Mississippi, and South Georgia.

BS: *You were carrying a gun?*

DD: I was never a nonviolent person when it came to what was going on there. There was nothing that could get your attention faster than a pair of bright headlights coming upon you, in the dark, on a back road of the Deep South in 1962-63. You hoped it was a police car, but that wasn't a guaranteed thing either. They were some pretty bad dudes. I covered Selma for two years before anybody ever knew where Selma was. We would go into these places where there was a disturbance, and be the first newsperson on the ground. There wasn't television news. It hadn't been invented as far as covering spot news stuff. I was really glad to see those guys show up for some company. We had reporters who were assaulted. It got pretty violent at times, and I testified against the sheriff in Selma in a federal trial.

BS: *What was the case?*

DD: I don't know the case. It had to be something about civil rights. I honestly don't know. There had been a huge riot, and he had called in the mounted posse, which was every asshole who had a horse in Clarke County, Alabama. They showed no mercy. I saw them stand a deputy on each arm of a black guy while a third guy would kick his ribs in and bloody heads all over the place. I tried to stay neutral in my reporting. Just the facts, and that was a good training ground for that, but I had to admit it would scare the daylights out of me sometimes. I mean, I didn't want to wear a hardhat, which was common then because that made me a target.

One day there was a crowd, a demonstration in downtown Selma, and the sheriff's deputies waded in. I stepped into a telephone booth that was in front of the courthouse. Those were the old Superman kind of telephone booths. I closed the doors, and the fight is just raging around outside. I called Atlanta to dictate my story, and suddenly this big deputy kicks open the door, and he says, what are you doing? I'm calling my company. I'm making a telephone call. And he says, did the sheriff say you could make that call? I said, does the sheriff own the telephone company? He hauled off with his nightstick and started to hit me. I punched him and took off, and I ended up in the sheriff's offices, which was nearby. I didn't think he would chase me in there. One of the sergeants had seen the episode and started laughing, and that cooled down. I pretty much wore out my welcome in Selma before it really got publicized.

BS: *Two questions. Did you get stopped on a dark road and you needed to use your gun? Did you meet Dr. King?*

DD: The first question, I carried my gun in my glove compartment, and I would have never stopped on a dark road.

BS: *Never?*

DD: Never. I never had to use the gun, just having it, needing the comfort of it, knowing that it was there in case things got worse. If they ever asked me where you from, boy? I would say I'm from further south than you. My grandfather was a member of the clan for Christ's sake.

I met Dr. King a number of times. He was always hustling around. Another one of those tight times was to be listening and covering a speech by Dr. King in a black church somewhere in Alabama and waiting for a stick of dynamite to come through the window. It was that kind of tenseness. You know the clan's outside. You never knew what those idiots would be up to.

BS: *That is scary.*

DD: I met all those guys. I was just one of a number. I was a low guy on the totem pole, and I had the privilege of working with some talented people. I learned from them. One of the things was to get the hell out of there.

BS: *Get out of Selma?*

DD: No to get out of Alabama.

BS: *Oh, the whole state.*

DD: The St. Petersburg Times hired me in Florida. Somebody asked me why are you moving to St. Pete? I said because my wife is pregnant, and I didn't want my son growing up with the stigma of being born in Alabama. I got along really well with Governor George Wallis, though. Cause, I was a daily reporter, you know one of the locals. We saw him every day, and every time he went into the song and dance about the pointy-headed social engineers from the north, he was talking about the guys from Milwaukee and New York. I would be in his office the very next day. I sat by him while he held a clemency hearing for a murderer. I flew seated right across the aisle from him when he would go on a trip to make a speech. He was thinking about running for president. I was in his office quite a bit because my boss at the time, a wonderful loud monster named Don Martin, who was a crazy man. He was a drunk womanizer from the word go, and he played golf like a pro. He taught me a lot. But it was just time for me to go.

BS: *That's when you went to St. Petersburg?*

DD: With St. Petersburg, I was a general assignment reporter. They liked me, and I liked them. I probably would have stayed there, but I think this is key that after traveling the back roads and getting my taste of the action, I got bored again. While I enjoyed it, it was awfully slow, and UPI called about that time and offered me a job in Miami. I took it, and so we moved down there. Two weeks later, St. Petersburg called me and asked me to come back and offered a $60 a week raise. That was big money back in those days. If they had given me that money in the first place, I would still be there. So, I rolled the dice and said, no, I'm going to stay with UPI and see what happens. That's when we got into the Cuba stuff with Castro and these very strange Cuban men who would come in at night and give you news releases about the big revolution.

BS: *Were they giving you Castro's side of the story?*

DD: No, this was the opposition, the spooks, the CIA paid guys. They were supposed to do the fighting, but all they did was march around in the everglades with broomsticks. Drugs had not hit yet. Miami was still a sleepy kind of place. After a year there, I landed right next to some of the real stars in the business. I regularly got amazed at the talented people at UPI that made me want to strive to get better. They expected excellence.

BS: *The people I've talked to are amazing. They are different, a cut above. I get it.*

DD: Later on, when I was hiring people, I would hire them based on the experience of little newspapers, show me some writing, but you also had to have some fire in your eyes. I wanted them lean and hungry. From there, I went to Richmond, Virginia, and made the mistake of becoming a state manager. Here again, locked in with the three guys that worked with me, my staff all went on to become much higher in the profession. One became a UPI vice president. One became a manager in Pittsburgh, and the third became the manager in the Washington, DC division. Talk about trying herd cats, we did a really good job, and it was a pleasure to watch them work.

I learned from them too. I was there for almost three years. I had been campaigning all this time to go to Vietnam. They wouldn't send me because I had a wife and children. They wouldn't send people with spouses because one of our reporters had gotten killed, and they had become responsible for the family. It had been a bad scene. You couldn't have dependents. I got divorced, and as soon as I did, I became eligible, and bye-bye Richmond, hello New York. That put me in touch with the people on the cable desk because I was ticketed for a foreign assignment. I had to learn all that, and the city staff, and the general run of people coming through New York. By this time, I had pretty much gotten to know everybody in UPI.

BS: *You'd been around.*

DD: Yes, I had been around. But, while I was still in Richmond, I got tabbed to cover a couple of the space shots. We would watch the rockets take off from the Cape, and then fly out to Houston, and I got to know some of the guys covering that, and I even met my best friend there. Ken Englade was the manager in New Mexico, and he was a full-fledged Cajun. He was my roomy on the space shots. I did Apollo 10, which was the one right before the moon landing, and then I went back and did the moon landing, too. Ken and I were given the task of reporting the first words of the man on the moon.

We were in an office with a couple of big tape recorders and headsets, and we had the president of UPI over one shoulder and an editor over another shoulder. We're sitting there like a couple of dolts with Remington typewriters waiting for Neil Armstrong to speak, and when he did, we got that 'one small step for man,' and we rattled that out. Ken was doing the same thing that I was doing right across the desk, and a bunch of other people in another room were doing the same thing. I think the whole damn world was trying to figure out what he was going to say. And then he said, 'one small step for man and one,' and then there was a level change in the audio coming into our booth, and we got the one small step for man and then garbled sound. I looked at Ken, and he looked at me and said, what that hell did he say? You talk about pressure, luckily though we got it. By the time we got the copy over to the desk, they already had it figured out. We had probably twenty of the best people in UPI working that shot. That was an interesting moment, and later in life, one of my books would be the life story of Gene Cernan, the last man to walk on the moon, which I had watched take off on Apollo 10. Strange, how he later came back in my life, and we became good friends.

Then I went off to Vietnam. I absolutely loved it. I thought of old Dr. Kopp back then, and I said okay Kopp, I paid attention in your damn course, and here I am. What an inspiration he was. I got there, and I was with what I considered the cream of the crop. In my biased opinion, every reporter worth his or her salt had to have Vietnam in their portfolio at that time. You had to have been able to say, yea, I was there. I got there, and I felt at home immediately.

One of our female reporters, by the name of Kate Webb, was captured by the Vietcong, and she was later released. She spent about seventeen days in the jungle as a prisoner. She was an Aussie and was quiet as could be. The natives just loved her. She would give them the shirt off her back. She was a tiger as far as being a reporter. That's one of the things, add that to the competition factor of working against AP in Saigon out in the field. Every story you had a minute by minute competition and that increased the stakes.

BS: *They're making a movie about her. What was it like in Vietnam? Did you go out on daily runs with the troops?*

DD: Remember, it was a helicopter war, and we were civilians. We were credited to the army, so we had all the permissions. In those days, we could go anywhere we wanted to go. You could hop either on a plane or catch a series of helicopters, and we could leave Saigon early in the morning, go out, find a battle somewhere, cover the event, and be back at 5 pm for the briefing, and listen to the army lie about it. It was a peculiar situation.

By the time we were there, Nixon was pulling out the Americans. It was that transition arc, the Vietnamization of the war. Vietnam was going to take over fighting its war, and we knew that it couldn't work. You would abandon a firebase somewhere and turn it over to the Vietnamese. The next day there would be chickens running around, laundry hanging on lines, and families living in the hooches. Military discipline was gone. The only thing that made it viable was American airpower. So, I stayed out with American troops as much as I could.

BS: *Were you ever in danger?*

DD: I didn't think so. There were tight scrapes, and I picked up a piece of shrapnel from a mortar shell, but not what I would consider a danger. That's where we wanted to be. It was much more fun to be huddled in the ditch than getting drunk in a Saigon bar. The gunfire was almost incidental. I flew with the air cab a lot, and I would get to know people who got shot down or get shot. Up near the DMZ one day, I spent a lot of time with a guy who had a shaggy dog. We were under pretty heavy artillery. We timed it. They were throwing an average of one shell at us every three seconds. There's not much you can do but sit there in the bunker, and hope for the best, because those things explode, and spread shrapnel the size of Volkswagen doors. My jeep had a flat tire nearby, and I was waiting for a lull to change it. Changing a tire when you're under fire is not a lot of fun. I got back to Saigon two days later and got the news that my new friend had just gotten blown up. One of those shells took out him and the dog. That was all part of the process. I would stay out for weeks at a time and come back to Saigon, get a change of clothes, and hang out for a while, and go somewhere else. I could go on forever about that.

BS: *Understood.*

DD: I had been the bureau's assistant manager, and finally, I was asked to take over as bureau manager. I said no, I didn't want to do that. Just let me do what I'm doing. The Saigon government had other ideas for me. The bureau manager was out at the time, he was on R&R, and the office manager, the local guy, came in and got me early in the morning after I had a buttery croissant and some delicious coffee at my desk. Make no mistake; the French left behind a whole bunch of really wonderful cooks. Those people knew how to cook. Our diplomatic/field reporter was the incredible Tracy Wood. Tracy runs a thing called OC Orange or something out in Los Angeles now, and she was a bubbly bright blonde in a miniskirt and an outstanding reporter. She handled the diplomat side. The rest of us weren't right for public consumption, so Tracy had to keep track of what was going on the political side. She would get out in the field too and got shot at. As part of her job, she had hired a beautiful French cook. She would bring leftovers from her little house parties to feed the bureau. It was that kind of croissant that I was eating the morning this guy came to get me. He said, "Monsieur Gunslinger."

BS: *Gunslinger?*

DD: Gunslinger, because I wore a black cowboy hat, and had a mustache. I don't know how it got there, but somebody named me that. The Vietnamese called me that. He says there's a dead body in the backyard. I said really and followed him back to the bathroom on the third floor, and stood on the tub, and sure enough, there was a corpse down in the courtyard. A burglar had tried to break in, lost his footing, and spiraled down to his death. Ain't no big deal - just another body. I said, okay call the white mice, that's what we called the local police because they wore white hats. As soon as I said that the office manager said you've got a telephone call from the foreign ministry. So, I stepped over to his desk, and the foreign ministry spokesman was calling me to tell me that I was going to be expelled from Vietnam, and I should be there about one o'clock or something for a meeting. I said okay and hung up the phone and walked back down the hall towards the news office. When I opened the door, there was the reporter from England for one of our biggest British clients down on his hands and knees trying to catch a rat in a trash can. I said, all of this before nine o'clock in the morning. It's just going to be that kind of day. That was the day they threw me out.

BS: *Why did they throw you out of the country?*

DD: The official version was biased, distorted, and inaccurate reporting. I said that's pretty vague. They didn't give any examples, just a broad brush. I was just the first example during the coming months. They were trying to clamp some controls on the press. The Vietnamese were taking over the war, and they made the rules. They were losing. Ironically, I had already scheduled dinner that night with a Colonel, the South Vietnamese army spokesman who announced my expulsion at the briefing that day, and we had dinner that night. He said you want to know why you're really getting thrown out? I said yea. I hadn't done anything that anybody else hadn't done. He said you ask too many questions. I said okay, Colonel, it's your show, and I bade him goodbye.

I wouldn't give anything for that experience. And now, UPI had to figure out what to do with me. They sent me to Hong Kong. It was our Asian headquarters.

BS: *I have a picture of you from 1971. You are "posing with two US soldiers at a firebase in Vietnam." You've got this kind of smirky, happy face. Do you remember that photo?*

DD: Yeah, I remember that photo. Dave Kennerly took it. He was a UPI photographer who won a Pulitzer Prize. I hate that photo because my hair is flying all over the place. That smile shows I had a good time. I got serious when I had to, but I was enjoying my people. Give me another bunch of correspondents, and I was a happy camper. Which then takes us back to Hong Kong. The main watering hole in Asia was the Hong Kong Foreign Correspondents Club. Them sending me to Hong Kong was like throwing the rabbit into the briar patch, exactly where I wanted to be, and I made friends with a whole bunch of people. The boss there was Bob

Page, he ran the business side for UPI throughout Asia, and he had been from Boston. He was one of the early Bostoners. Again, I'm in a good mix of topflight journalists. We had a great staff, and my days at the Foreign Correspondents Club, or the FCC as we called it, were delightful. I could not go back to Vietnam. All my pals from Vietnam, Cambodia, and Laos would come back and would circulate through the bar. I could still go to Cambodia, but I couldn't go to Vietnam. So, by accident again, I'm forced back into management. Instead of being a field reporter with the tanks and the shooting, I'm at a desk again shuffling papers, and worrying about other people's workdays.

Through some inner workings there we had a change of my boss. The news manager for Asia left and lo and behold, a fellow by the name of Al Webb comes in. He's a freaking legend in UPI. He was a brilliant writer, and he was a total drunk and a kook. He should have been kept in a cage somewhere. He had covered the early space shots and spent time in Vietnam and gotten a medal for bravery from the Marine Corp during the Battle of Hue. Then, he went to Europe. I was told I wasn't old enough for the opening for the manager job in Asia, and so they picked Al. Boy, was I ever happy about that. First, I didn't have to do the job, and second, Webb was a legend. He came back, and it felt like I was back in Atlanta UPI for the first day. I was in charge of basically running the far-flung bureaus and was assigning people to New Delhi or Singapore. All the names I had grown up worshiping like Leon Daniel, for example, were people I was assigning. These incredible reporters, writers, and even my former friends down in Vietnam, I just liked these guys so much, and I loved handling their copy that kept flowing in from all points. We'd file it on to New York. With Webb there to run the show, it was like a doctor you got an advanced course in journalism hanging around Al Webb. Everybody had an Al Webb story. The secret to our line of work was you had to be able to pack a lot of information into very few words. A UPI story was built on the inverted pyramid. What was useful to a newspaper in one town had to be cut from the bottom to even get in the newspaper. You tried to make every paragraph interesting with a hook to read the next paragraph. It was an art all its own, and Webb was a master of it. Al liked cats. He had three cats that he kept with him all the time.

**BS:** *At work?*

**DD:** He didn't bring them to work often, but he had been known to do it. He lived in one of those high-rise apartments in Hong Kong. One day a cat fell off. He was so morose. The rumor going around was the cat committed suicide from living with Webb.

In assigning transfers, I brought in my friend Ken Englade. He followed me from Hong Kong. I brought Tracy Wood in, and I brought in Sylvana Foa, who later became a honcho with the United Nations, and, of course, we had Joe Galloway who wrote the story about the Battle of the la Drang Valley. He wrote the book *We Were Soldiers Once...and Young.* They made it into a movie starring Mel Gibson. So, Galloway was just one of the team. I could go on forever with the team. This was the leftovers with the gang from Vietnam. What do you do with these people? You can't leave everybody in Saigon, so we farmed them out to faraway places, and luckily, they were still there when Saigon fell.

But back to the story. I'm managing again and not doing a very good job of it. An opening comes in Boston. I wanted to go to Europe, but I made the mistake of falling in love with a girl from Boston. And Bob Page was from Boston. He gets a great idea, let's transfer Davis to Boston. He'll be happy. He can help out there. Also, I wanted to get away from Hong Kong because so many of my really good friends fell into what I call the Hong Kong 'trap,' and that was to become an expatriate and a full-fledged drunk. You're a single white man in paradise with a generous expense account. Why leave? I actually had friends that died standing at the bar of the Hong Kong Foreign Correspondents Club. We even had one die in the men's room while he was on the toilet. I had never been to Boston, but my girlfriend was a nurse, and we were going to settle down. So, I've expanded on the excitement and how much I enjoyed life in Asia. Right?

**BS:** *Right, I got it.*

**DD:** Suddenly I move from wild and woolly Asia to a soft ivy league existence. I'm saying, what the fuck? The only exciting thing that happened during my first week there was I got mugged on the Boston Common. I think I arrived there in about 1974. I was going through the metamorphosis of what am I doing here, and having to make all new friends, and get used to a whole new system. The first thing I discovered; they didn't need me there at all. They had a fine crew. A fellow named Jim Wieck was the news center editor. Bernie Caughey was the division news manager, and Bill Ketter had taken over the sales thing. UPI had owned New England. We dominated that dog ass Associated Press. Two weaknesses developed. The staff could do the job. It was a rich hunting ground when you went looking for recruits. It was structurally a problem. About a year before, they had created a system to save money called the news center concept, where we assigned people to write radio copy instead of being out originating it. Their reporting skills were wasted.

BS: *So not originating stories, merely rewriting them for newspapers?*

DD: The six states in our region would originate the stories from there end and feed them into Boston. Boston would handle it, and then we would take it, and send it out to the newspapers. We had responsibilities to send regular stories out 24/7 to radio and television clients. This is where it fell off the rails. It required a lot of punching into the keyboards and writing to feed those stories in small packages hour after hour. There are only so many ways you can say a story. That machine kept going. It took the props away for a lot of local reporting. It didn't take a genius to see that. This was the computer age just coming in, and easy to shift stories around. It was electrons and words. It wasn't really serious writing like we used to do like I had grown up on in Atlanta. The question was, were we covering Boston? I'm the new Boston bureau manager, and you would think I would cover Boston, and the answer is no. This is where Ketter, Page, and Caughey came in. They had made a deal with some of the subscribers to pay a special fee to hire two news reporters who would solely have the job of being investigative reporters at the statehouse in Massachusetts. We had two people up there already, and now we have four.

BS: *That doesn't sound like UPI. They were so cheap they would never over hire.*

DD: Yeah, keep that in mind as we go along here. So, now we have the deal to have two general reporters and two investigative reporters fully assigned. Those four people were located across the street from us in Ashburton Place. They didn't play by the same rules as us. They might as well have been on the moon, and they became a little kingdom. They grew closer over the years, and we got the inevitable result, which was the lack of Massachusetts' original coverage with hardly anything out of Boston, and very few exposes.

BS: *What were they doing?*

DD: That's a damn good question, and I don't have the answer still today. They would spend the day over there and come in at night and drop off reams and reams of copy that was middle of the road at best. They had a real Boston elitist attitude. They forgot they were working for a 24/7 wire service, in my opinion. That would prove to be part of our downfall. We hardly covered anything happening in Boston. We didn't need a Rolodex because we didn't do anything.

If there were something big, there would be all troops on deck, like a big blizzard, or a natural disaster, or the pope comes to town. I had to file a request to borrow people from the statehouse team because they were the investigators, to put them out on the damn street to cover the critical stories. Whenever I would send people over there to relieve them, I would pick one of my young and hungry ones to get experience, and just let time take care of the problem. They wouldn't even file radio briefs. When I tried to take one, I would get yelled at from the other side. We contractually had to keep them over there. It was a no-win situation. And so, I focused on what we could do, and let them run their show, but I kept an eye on it. They were off-limits for general reporting. Meanwhile, I've got news breaking out there that I can't get to. Luckily, I had begun to hire a lot of people, and move them around to different bureaus. These kids had the spirit. It was a rich hiring environment.

BS: *It's Boston. It's educated.*

DD: Not only for the talent for a new hire, but they also had to be on fire. They had to want to make a touchdown. And, eventually, they did. Eileen McNamara later won a Pulitzer Prize with the Boston Globe. Andy Nibley became the head of Reuters. We had guys who became lawyers and doctors. I had MIT graduates. Plus, the guys, like good old Dave Haskell, who was my rock, and an incredible asset. I could always depend on Dave to keep them straight.

One day, I was in Washington at the White House, and there were in the White House press room, maybe twenty people. Just an ordinary day before a briefing. And six people in that press room had New England and Boston roots. I said goddamn, we must have been doing something right up there. A lot of them went on to outstanding careers elsewhere, and I managed to keep a lot of them running New England bureaus. So, the team was pretty much in place, and if I did anything, I think I just lit a fire under them, showed them some of the basics. You're not just some soft team; you're elite. You're good. You can cover anything. But I was back to being a manager, and I was about to be a bigger manager when Bernie went to New York.

When Saigon fell in 1975, I was beside myself. I was in Boston, and I hated being there, I wanted to be back there on the street, with my buddies. Bernie scolded me pretty hotly to make up my mind, and become a normal human being again, or wander around Asia. I almost said I'm going to wander around Asia. I had a good deal. I recognized that. I got to the point where the low pay and the conditions of UPI were getting to me, and I did not like managing other people. I wanted to get back to reporting and writing. That's where I was happiest. After that, I began looking for the right exit off the Expressway. It took a couple of years. Many things were happening. We had the Bicentennial, which was great fun, and we had the blizzards, and sports were always big in Boston. The madness in early spring, you had the Red Sox playing, the Celtics, the Bruins if they were in the playoffs, plus the Marathon, and it all hit at the same weekend. The place went sort of screwy. My focus was the entire region when Bernie left, but I had some star bureau managers in New England.

You're playing with equals. We didn't have a bunch of rookies. They just kept getting better, and I took great pride in that. I knew I could do the job. Could the guys and gals coming up behind me do the job? Training them, putting them in place, and seeing them go on to do magnificent things with their lives was a real kick for me.

BS: *I get it.*

DD: I had crossed swords with HL Stevenson, my boss in New York. He was the editor. Steve and I went back a long way. He hired me in Atlanta, and HL Stevenson was the boss. He helped me a lot over the years. We became good friends, but he was a, how do I put this, Steve was a hard boss. He ran a lot of people off, that plus the low pay. There came a time when the managing editor of UPI retired or quit. The call went out for the division news editors to go to New York to be interviewed. I refused to go, and that pissed him off. I wasn't happy being a manager. I knew I could do the job and do it pretty well. And I probably would have enjoyed it.

One, I didn't want to live in New York on a UPI salary and two, Steve was becoming such a martinet that the last guy before the morning news conferences would go into the bathroom, stick his finger down his throat, and throw up because he was so nervous that Steve was going to jump all over him. Steve wanted a yes man, and that wasn't me. We agreed to disagree.

There was a big battle going on way above my head. It was the Bob Page way of managing, and the Stevenson way. Both wanted to be president. Depending on whose camp you were in defined what your prospects were. I was in both camps. Page from Asia and Stevenson was Steve. I didn't want to take sides, but I would have leaned toward Page because Page was saner. I also recognized that there wasn't much to save at UPI then. He gave me an ultimatum and that I could go to Moscow, and eventually take over London, or I could go to Washington. I said okay, I'll go to Washington, and I'll give it a try.

BS: *Before you go there, did you marry the girl that you went to Boston for?*

DD: Yes. That was Chris. She was my second wife. My first one, Pam, was in Virginia. I've changed wives almost as often as I changed shoes. I couldn't help it. I fell in love with almost every woman I met.

BS: *Okay, that's funny. You're in Washington.*

DD: I moved down to Washington, and I immediately have a serious illness in May of 1981. I remember the date because that was the same day that Ronald Reagan was shot. He's in the hospital somewhere else, and I'm packed in ice bags because I've got a temperature of 105. I had a bad kidney infection.

Back at work, I was on the desk again. Everybody considered that a demotion, but I didn't give a damn, because I had my eyes on the White House, and I eventually got that. I had made up my mind. I wanted to write books, damn it. And I was not getting any closer to it by sticking around UPI. Chris and I were divorced, and I needed the pay to raise my kids.

BS: *You're single again and looking for your next, next wife.*

DD: On my first trip to California, on Air Force One with Ronald Reagan, I got off the plane, and I saw a girl waiting down there in my favorite color scheme, which was black leather, and red hair. That was Robin. She was doing PR for the city of Santa Barbara. We hooked up, and I covered Reagan for a few years and loved working with Helen Thomas and Sam Donaldson. We had a good crew. But, it was pretty much, been there, done that. I enjoyed the stint but, that was a temporary thing as far as I was concerned. Robin was a vice president of a political consulting company, and we carried on a long-distance relationship for about a year. By this time, UPI was falling apart. The writing was on the wall. I got out while the getting was good. She quit her job, and I left my job and went to San Diego, California. I got a job as a columnist and political writer for the San Diego Union, with the bonus, they let me run around Asia a lot. I had a new position, the Pacific Rim reporter. The company had money. So, I went everywhere from Beijing to Sydney. They let me roam and do a lot of things. This allowed me to put things on hold while my two sons, Russ, and Randy, grew up. In 1990, I said, okay, I'm tired of this news stuff, and so we kicked over the checkerboard one more time and moved to Colorado to write books.

BS: *You have a lot of books to your name.*

DD: My old buddy Ken Englade was in New Mexico. He had started doing true crime books. He had been in touch with our editor in New York and wanted me to do one. He couldn't do the book, and said to them try Davis, he just quit, and he could give it a go. And I did. The book turned out to be about young Jeffrey Dahmer, the cannibal of Milwaukee. I wrote that book in about 60 days. It was really easy. I knew how to work fast, and it became my first NY Times bestseller. I said, wow, this is pretty easy. I like this. After that, I averaged a book a year for the next twenty or thirty-something years. That was published in 1990, and I've had a book a year since then.

BS: *Some of the other books you wrote about included OJ Simpson.*

DD: I hit the true-crime circuit before television discovered it as reality TV. Those books did really well. We'd print a half million of them. I came in just as the big four hit the nineties: Dahmer, OJ Simpson, the Menendez brothers, and JonBenet Ramsay. I hit a grand slam because I did books on all of them.

BS: *What happened to JonBenet?*

DD: First of all, we got sued for $80 million. I think it was. I wrote that book with Steve Thomas, who was the lead investigator, and Steve was gold about it. We knew whoever wrote the ransom note killed the kid, and mommy wrote the ransom note. Brush away all the other evidence that's who killed the kid. We got sued because Steve had to go on doing publicity. He went on the Larry King Show and told Patsy Ramsey to her face that he liked her for the murder. They didn't get anything. They got a couple of thousand bucks to settle out of court. We wanted to go to trial. We would have kept her on the stand for days. We had lawyers lined up across the nation wanting to take that case. There was never a problem, and we never retracted a word.

BS: *The other name that sticks out to me is Isoroku Yamamoto.*

DD: He was the guy who planned Pearl Harbor.

BS: *I had no idea until I read the recap on the book.*

DD: He was the military heart and soul of the Japanese empire. Some Americans shot him down, and there was a great controversy about who shot him down, and how. I wrote a book on that called *Lightning Strike* and talked personally with dozens of men who served on Guadalcanal. I went to their conventions and things like that. They were a great help to put this to rest. The book did pretty well. It wasn't a bestseller, but it was a good book.

BS: *Tell me about Shooter.*

DD: Let's tackle that one last, and I'll throw in a couple more here. The last man on the moon book, Gene Cernan, was an autobiography, and he couldn't get the right kind of writer to work for him. I wanted to get out of the true-crime business as lucrative as it had been.

The agent put me together with Gene, and I flew down to Houston. We met, and we liked each other instantly, and the fact that I had actually seen him take off for his Apollo shot turned the corner. Gene poured his heart into this. He really wanted to get it right. He said I want you to put the reader on top of the rocket with me. But my favorite image of Gene is not him walking on the moon, but him lying on my sofa with my hound dog over his feet reading pages of copy. He just died a couple of months ago and was a great man. He really was unique. Getting to know him showed me how competitive those guys were. Through him, I got to meet most of the astronauts and the supporting team, so I enjoyed that.

There was another book called *Dark Waters*, the story of the NR-1, the navy's smallest nuclear submarine, which was a spy boat. My co-author was one of the original crew members. We walked that story of the NR-1 from the drawing board, all the way through construction, to the first of four captains. It was just fascinating. This little submarine would crawl around on the floor of the ocean on Goodyear truck tires to snip Russian cables. That was a fun one to write.

I would write other books with other people as they came along, and I would ghost-write. I did one called *Kill Bin Laden*, which was a bestseller. It was done with the commander of the Delta Force troops that went after bin Laden, in Afghanistan, in the very first days of the conflict. I did one on the crazy prophet, Warren Jeffs, who married 28 little girls. Writing fulfilled my need for action. You never knew what was coming next—a good ride overall.

Along came *Shooter*. A marine sniper by the name of Jack Coughlin was my co-author and Casey Kuhlman, who was a captain. When the first Gulf war was over, and people were tying yellow bands around trees to welcome home troops, here comes Jack back to the United States, a top sniper in the marine corp. His wife meets him at the airport with divorce papers and says, "here's the two girls and good luck." Suddenly he can't raise two girls on a marine's sergeant salary. He decides to write a book with his pal Casey. Just because you have a story, doesn't mean you know how to write. I said earlier, in the news business, you learn to write tight. You do the opposite with books. You've got a 90,000-word canvas to fill up. It's a hard job. The agents put us together, and we wrote the story of one marine's adventures during the first Gulf war. Luckily for us, his unit had gone from the first charge, all the way through to where Jack was lying on the grass in central square when his unit helped pull down the Saddam Hussein statue. He had it all. The book did very well.

BS: *It's a New York Times bestseller also.*

DD: Yeah, it was. At that time, the editor and I said the character here is too good. Military superheroes were coming online in interest, and all these soldiers were coming back. Everybody has a story, and everybody loves snipers. We decided to make a fictional sniper character, and we started a series based loosely on Jack as a person. That damn thing took off.

BS: *Your book, Shooter, was the biography, and then you went on to write ten more fictionalized versions.*

DD: Yes, with Jack and me as co-authors. When you're dealing with a military audience, you get to know that shit, and they will call you on any of the slightest details. It worked. After ten, I said that's enough, and here we sit today.

BS: *What are you working on now?*

DD: Nothing. Because I'm 79 years old and I'm tired.

BS: *Come on, Don. You're only 79.*

DD: It's the eyes. I do have one book bouncing around right now about the second Korean war. I sit around and make shit up. It's great fun.
   One of my faults and I have many, is I never liked doing the publicity.

I didn't like the talk show circuit. You flew around and spent a lot of time in K-Marts. They put you at a card table and hope somebody buys a book. The best time I had was at the National Air and Space Museum with Gene Cernan. We were sitting beneath Charles Lindbergh's plane, and the line went out the door and around the block. They're not all like that. Writing is a hard business, and promoting it is even worse. I recognized early on how to make this work; I had to be a small businessman first and a creative artist second.

That's all I have. You pretty much picked me clean. My time in Boston was invaluable. I learned that you could not please everybody. Some are gonna love you, and some are gonna hate you. It's just the way the dice rolls. I think I left it in a better place with a little more spark and energy. But like I said, they were doing fine.

## Chapter 12

---

### Richard C. Gross—Rolodex Connection:
### UPI Editor and Reporter

---

*Anwar Sadat and Menachem Begin, Love at 77*

Richard C. Gross has impeccable journalism credentials. Among his experiences are UPI reporter in Boston, UPI Bureau manager in Israel, Pentagon correspondent, and opinion page editor for the Baltimore Sun. He covered Anwar Sadat's visit to Jerusalem, the Delta Force invasion of Grenada, and reported from all over the globe. He preferred to respond to questions about his career through email.

BS: *I'd like to start from the beginning, where are you from?*

RG: I was born March 10, 1940, to immigrant parents in the East Bronx in a neighborhood close to my mother's parents. When I was 18 months old, my parents moved to a one-bedroom apartment on the second floor of a six-story red and white brick building in the West Bronx, in walking distance of New York University and its Hall of Fame. I knew nothing of it. We moved to a two-bedroom fourth-floor apartment in the same building when I was nine. So much for instability in my early years. My brother, Donald, two years, ten months younger than I, shared a room. That was tough at times.

My father, Joseph, an émigré from what is now Slovakia, was a dental technician. He and his younger brother, Arpad, worked together in a lab in Manhattan's Union Square, about a 45-minute train ride from our station, 183rd Street. They split April 1, 1956, when I was 16, and he wound up with his own lab in that location while my uncle moved uptown to another one near Times Square. My mother, who emigrated from Romania, was a housewife, raising two boys.

My most memorable public school experience came in eighth grade when my teacher, Mrs. Murphy, told us to write a short story as a home-work assignment. I loved the idea. I wound up writing 26 legal pad pages longhand, a story I called "The Lost Island of Atlantis." I was a science-fiction fan at the time. And I read nothing else, stupidly. However, that short story sparked my interest in writing, led to my buying a portable Royal typewriter when I was in high school, and I used it to tap out more short stories that I submitted to pulp sci-fi magazines for publication. Nothing ever came of it, but a pile of rejection slips. Heck, I was only a kid. My parents never encouraged me though they never complained about the noise I was making typing at night.

I did not go to college after graduation from high school in 1958. I didn't like high school, was bored with classes, did not get good grades in school, and certainly was not an academic. I had no idea what I wanted to do with myself. I was lost.

I got a job as a runner in a Wall Street brokerage house, Ira Haupt & Co., at 120 Broadway, for $40 a week. It was the summer after my high school graduation. I was promoted to a clerk position in the Purchase & Sales Department. I knew deep down I didn't want to be a Wall Street clerk for the rest of my life. I decided to enroll at night school at City College of New York; it was free. It was the end of the workday, and again, I had no interest in classroom learning.

A girlfriend, at the time, saw something that I didn't know existed in myself. She pushed me to go to college away from the city. She rode up with me to Springfield, Mass., to check out American International College, a private school of about 1,100 in western Massachusetts. I liked what I saw, applied, and was accepted. I entered AIC in September 1961, when I was 21.

For some reason, maybe because of the short story writing, maybe because of my experience on the high school newspaper, I joined the weekly college paper, *The Yellow Jacket*, and immediately started writing a column called "What Would Happen If . . . ," a takeoff on my years of reading sci-fi. It didn't seem to move any needles of appreciation on campus, though that didn't occur to me at the time. Then, out of the blue, I wrote a column satirizing the drug store across State Street from the college, focusing on how long it took to be served lunch. Lots of kids must have had the same lunch experience at that place because the column became a hit, and I suddenly became known. I had never been "known" before. Fame, I loved the attention. It's what I needed most in life. But who knew? So, welcome to Journalism 101. Unfortunately, AIC did not have a journalism department.

I continued writing the column, and the staff elected me editor of the YJ, as it was called, my junior and senior years. I blossomed. I was features editor of the yearbook, *The Taper*. I wrote short stories for and was features editor of the literary magazine, *The Criterion*. I wrote the books for two musical comedies, Campus Capers, that were produced onstage at school. The flood of extracurricular activities kept me from my studies, but I did manage to graduate in June 1965 with a bachelor's in English and a minor in history, if not with honors.

It was enough to get me an assistantship that Fall to the chairman of the journalism department, David Manning White, at the Boston University School of Public Communications. I was studying for a master's in journalism, but a degree wasn't to be because I became a reporter for *The Boston Traveler*, the evening newspaper of The *Boston Herald*.

The job came out of the blue. I had been manning the journalism school desk when the phone rang, and it was Steven Dunleavy, an editor at the Traveler who was recruiting students to write for the paper's new School Page. It meant working part-time in the evenings covering meetings of various suburban school committees. I told Dunleavy, "What about me?" So began my journalism career.

The Traveler took me on full time as its education reporter later that school year, in 1966, at $80 a week. Since I had a job as a reporter, what was the point of going to journalism school? I quit without getting a degree. As a cub reporter, I was covering the biggest story in Boston: Louise Day Hicks of the Boston School Committee and her opposition to busing black students in Roxbury to white schools in the southern part of the city, known as Southie, an Irish area. I was getting banner headlines.

BS: *Who hired you at UPI?*

RG: Great as it was, I left my post at the Traveler to follow a rumor that UPI in Boston was looking for a reporter. I went to its shoddy office on

State Street, a long row of teletype machines banging away under a line of windows, and spoke with Stanton (Stan) Berens, the manager of the New England Division. He hired me immediately, mostly because of my experience at the Traveler. I got a $40 weekly raise, to $120. That was Feb. 27, 1967.

BS: *Who did you most admire on your way? Can you talk about the women that you worked with?*

RG: I most admired Berens because I respected him the most. There were no women in the 16-man Boston bureau at the time. The woman I most admired those years was the education reporter for *The Boston Herald*, the morning newspaper of the Traveler. Older and more experienced, she helped me learn the ins and outs of the education beat.

BS: *What was the Boston office location? Who did you work with?*

RG: The office first was situated on State Street, one of Boston's main drags near the Freedom Trail, and the financial and courthouse districts. It later moved to the Massachusetts Teachers Association building across the street from the State House, where I was a reporter for about two years.

I started the "newsman" job during daylight. I recall I ended the first story I wrote, on a two- or three-page copybook with carbon paper between the pages—with a typewriter, of course—with a --30--. I thought that was the universal way of ending a news story. But not at UPI. One ended it with one's initials if I recall.

I handed the copybook across two desks to the news editor for the morning, or AM, cycle, Guy Darst. He glanced at it, saw the ending, and threw it back to me across the desks, pages fluttering. "That's not how we end news stories," he barked. I never forgot his rudeness and, actually, never forgave him for it. He did mutter something like, "He can write." Yes, I could. Darst wound up as an editorial writer for *The Herald*, which had switched from a broadsheet to a tabloid.

I moved rapidly from the day desk to the nightside, which meant working from 4 pm until midnight. Barry Brooks, the State House reporter, quit several months after I arrived to go into public relations, which meant a living wage. Of all of the staffers in the bureau, Berens chose me to replace him. I was shocked and overwhelmed with joy. It would mean I would be a full-time reporter, not a desker. I think it was because he liked the way I write.

I went to cover the legislature with a desk at the State House. The UPI person I worked with most closely during the two years I was there—until August 1969—was bureau manager Paul Robbins. I reported directly to him. I worked a great deal of overtime, which certainly helped boost my pay. It also provided the opportunity to cover the New England delegations to the 1968 Democratic convention in Chicago—a tumultuous affair—and the Republican convention in Miami. I also covered Democratic and Republican candidates for the presidential nominations in New Hampshire. Of particular note was covering Democrat Eugene McCarthy and his capture of 42 percent of the vote in that state's primary, boosting him to national prominence as the peace candidate during some of the darkest days of the Vietnam War. The Tet offensive began in February 1968.

There always were far more men than women in journalism back in the '60s. When there were women, like UPI's Helen Thomas at the White House, they were restricted to writing about women things, like first ladies. It's sad. Lots of women now are excellent journalists.

BS: *You started in UPI Boston's bureau in 1968, the same year that Kevin White was elected to his first term. Would you reflect on him and the stories that you did covering him?*

RG: I don't recall covering him. Unless White said or did something of statewide or national interest, such as winning election as mayor, there would be no reason for a wire service to cover him. The two Boston Globes and the Herald and the Traveler covered Boston extensively.

BS: *In 1973, you were in Israel covering for UPI, the October War, the Yom Kippur War, also during Ramadan, Egypt and Syria attacked Israel. Describe your thoughts.*

RG: I was a staff correspondent when the war erupted on October 6, 1973, 17 months after I arrived in the country from a month of orientation in Brussels, then the headquarters for UPI's Europe, the Middle East, and Africa Division, or EUROMEDAF. Tom Cheatham, the bureau manager of UPI in Tel Aviv, where we were headquartered, called me at the home of my in-laws about a half hour's drive south of Tel Aviv, where my wife and I had gone for the Yom Kippur holiday. He asked me to come to the bureau because there were rumors that hostilities had begun with Egypt and Syria in a coordinated surprise attack. I picked up a soldier along the way who was hitchhiking to his base in Tel Aviv. Cheatham sent me immediately to the government press office on Kaplan Street, a two-minute walk from the bureau. The Israel Defense Force's spokesman's office also was in that building. Soldiers were rushing around. When I asked one of them what was going on, his response was, "It's a war." I immediately called that into Cheatham, who was manning the desk in the bureau.

Egyptian forces had crossed the Suez Canal into the Israeli-occupied Sinai Peninsula, overwhelming fortified Israeli barriers with the goal of recapturing the sandy desert territory. At the same time, Syrian tanks and armored units swept like a river across the Israeli-held Golan Heights. Their objective was to swarm down from the high ground, drive to the Mediterranean coast, and cut Israel in two. Israel captured both territories during the 1967 Middle East War.

I was in Tel Aviv one morning very early in the war and wrote a breaking story in which I dubbed the conflict the "October War, " searching for some middle ground between the Yom Kippur War and what the Arabs were calling the Ramadan War. One thing about a wire service: it goes everywhere, to newspapers and TV and radio stations. The October War label stuck.

After that first day in Tel Aviv, Cheatham dispatched me to all of the battlefields, beginning with the Golan Heights then into Sinai and then across the canal into Egypt as Israeli forces slowly pushed Egyptian and Syrian forces back in each theater of operations during the 18-day war. Fear was my companion each step of the way, more so because I never had been in the U.S. military and had no training in covering military operations. As if to prove my inexperience, I stupidly drove my Peugeot convertible in approaching darkness onto the Golan Heights battlefield, a soft vehicle as one could deploy into a war zone, the ground torn by shrapnel. I drove all the way across the Syrian line into Kuneitra, a battered city where I watched in a trench where Israeli troops wrestled with a Syrian soldier, his mouth in a grimace as he tried to fight off his captors, gold teeth glinting. I was mesmerized. The car and I survived as I drove back to northern Israel to call the bureau.

The biggest scare came a day or two later when I attached myself to a medevac unit in Syria proper. At one point, I sat in a U.S.-built half-track vehicle spooning army lunch rations out of a can, a gunner on the lookout above me. The gunner yelled, "MiG," and we all dived for cover as the jet swooped in toward us. In another stupid move, I dove under the target—the half-track—a huge old Sony tape recorder slung over one shoulder, a camera over the other. I gripped the bare, chocolate-colored earth with the fingers of both hands as the MiG strafed us with machine gunfire. I prayed for Israeli F-4 Phantoms to come to the rescue. The MiG rushed past, hitting nothing. Realizing my error in choosing where to hide, I rolled out from under the half-track and jumped into a nearby pile of rocks, banging up my left shoulder as I expected the MiG to return. He didn't. I later put the tape recorder to good use by doing a radio spot from inside a brand new abandoned Soviet-built Syrian T-72 tank for UPI's Audio division.

Once the Israelis secured the Golan, I was dispatched to the Sinai to cover the war there. The desert was littered with destroyed or abandoned Egyptian and Israeli tanks, also Soviet-made. Military checkpoints along the main coastal road kept reporters from getting to the front. The only action I saw was a photographer pouring gasoline over a damaged Israeli tank, setting it afire, and taking pictures of it to show back home that war indeed was flaming in the Sinai. What decades later would be referred to as "fake news" was in full bloom in 1973.

Once Israelis recaptured the Sinai, General Ariel Sharon sent his tanks and mechanized infantry across the Suez Canal on pontoon bridges on a quest to go after the Egyptian 3rd Army farther to the south. The Egyptians eventually were surrounded, with Israeli forces facing them in both the Sinai and Egypt. I never got to see any combat. A cease-fire was declared on October 22.

Anyone who believes war is a romantic exercise is a fool. It means death and destruction, with advanced weapons such as missiles worsening the devastation. No one goes onto a battlefield without a belly full of butterflies.

Egypt and Israel made peace in 1979, closing Israel's back door to invasion. As part of that pact, Israel surrendered the Sinai to Egypt in 1982, evacuating about 8,000 Jewish settlers. It left the Gaza Strip in 2005, which soon after was taken over by Hamas, which the United States has labeled a terrorist organization. Israel and Syria never made peace. Israel annexed the windswept Golan Heights in 1981.

Syria kept the cease-fire agreement along the frontier, but Israel today is wary about Iran spreading its influence in Syria and in neighboring Lebanon, where it controls the Shia militia, Hezbollah. Israeli warplanes have struck Iranian and Syrian targets in Israel in a sustained effort to ensure their forces stay deep into the Syrian interior and away from the Golan Heights. The Russians returned to Syria during its disastrous seven-year civil war. Israeli Prime Minister Benjamin Netanyahu met with Russian President Vladimir Putin several times to urge him to control both the Syrians and Iranians.

BS: *There's a stat that's reported, "Two-thirds of American millennials surveyed in a recent poll cannot identify what Auschwitz is," You lived in a time and covered stories that need to be told and retold.*

RG: The Holocaust, the calculated elimination of 6 million European Jews, is a singularly epic event not only in the history of the Jewish people but in the history of the world, the ultimate in ethnic cleansing by Nazi Germany during World War II. The overwhelming scale of the wanton annihilation of innocent men, women, and children with everything from bullets to gas chambers stands alone as a hallmark of the perpetration of evil in the annals of human existence. That two-thirds of 73 million millennials have no idea what Auschwitz was—the epitome of the mass execution of a people—is a crime and an indictment of the state of the American educational system today. It certainly is a comment on the intelligence and outlook of the American reading public.

I occasionally wondered when writing news stories that needed a paragraph of background explanation for nearly every paragraph of the breaking event, especially when writing from abroad for an American audience, whether anyone but a small minority gave a whit about what I was covering. I tried very hard to ensure that I put enough perspective into a complicated story so that the reader could grasp the significance of the event. Of course, it depended on the story. Covering the Bucharest earthquake of March 1977 didn't involve much depth or perspective since the story involved the numbers of dead and injured, its impact on survivors, the extent of the destruction, what it meant for the Romanian capital, whether there were threats of further quakes, etc.

It was far more complicated than writing about President Ronald Reagan's push to build a Star Wars defense in space, which he announced in March 1983. The announcement had far-reaching repercussions, to the billions of dollars it would cost, its impact on U.S. allies, what it meant in terms of standing up to Soviet military power, and whether such a program was feasible. Significantly, the background for the Star Wars initiative was the overall Reagan administration buildup of the military, beginning with a $181 billion supplemental Pentagon budget the president introduced in October 1981, ten months after he entered the office. I was covering the Pentagon at the time, a seven-year assignment. In the end, the program fizzled out after an expenditure of about $33 billion.

Star Wars may have been a mere blip in the history of the Pentagon, but it deserves its place in history because the program was dedicated to confronting the main adversary of the United States, the Soviet Union. Earthquakes come and go worldwide, and they do have an impact, many times a lasting one, but the U.S. competition with the Soviet Union is a significant piece of history that should not be forgotten.

BS: *I remembered having a deep respect for Anwar Sadat and was so saddened at his assassination. I was 27, and it seemed like the end of hope to me. Would you talk about his visit to Jerusalem?*

RG: To paraphrase in summary: One small step for a visionary Arab leader, one giant leap toward peace between Israel and its Arab neighbors.

Anwar Sadat's spellbinding visit to Jerusalem November 19, 1977, the first Arab leader to officially step foot in Israel, marked a dramatic, momentous historic turning point in relations between the Arab world and the Jewish state. He met with Israeli Prime Minister Menachem Begin and addressed the Knesset or parliament. Much of the Arab world vehemently opposed Sadat's startling outreach to a former enemy, who won four wars against Egypt in 1948-49, 1956, 1967, and 1973, the last being the October war.

"The October war should be the last war," Sadat said at the time.

"No more war, no more bloodshed," Begin said then.

I was the UPI bureau manager in Tel Aviv at the time, monitoring Sadat's arrival from Cairo, pounding out the main story and its subsequent updates to it on a typewriter while watching events unfold in Jerusalem on the black and white television. It marked the first time I wrote a story live as it happened, tearing pages from the typewriter and handing them to a staffer to punch my words into a yellow tape that was put into a transmitter that sent the copy to UPI in London, headquarters for our UPI division. I remember recalling how I watched, mouth agape, as UPI Washington staffer Tom Corpora wrote what UPI termed running copy, as politicians spoke from the podium of the 1968 Democratic convention in Chicago. I stood dumbfounded, thinking I never could do that. But nine years later, I did.

Sadat's bold and brave journey to Jerusalem and the events that were to follow leading to the signing of the Egyptian-Israeli peace treaty in March 1979 was the most significant story I covered during my four-decade career in daily journalism.

Sadat's brief visit put in motion a slew of events, including Begin's trip to Egypt, much of which was a sightseeing journey to such magnificent tourist sites as the ancient temple complex at Karnak, the pyramids, the Sphinx and the two huge rock temples at Abu Simbel at Lake Nasser. Egyptian and Israeli negotiators met at the Mena House in Cairo, in the shadow of the pyramids at Giza, for talks that would lead to the 13-day gathering at Camp David among President Jimmy Carter, Sadat, and Begin. I dubbed the agreements that were signed on September 17, 1978, the Camp David Accords. I believe I coined that label for the agreements; I hadn't seen it elsewhere before. The accords led to the signing in Washington of the Egyptian-Israeli peace treaty on March 26, 1979. I covered the signing, having traveled there with Begin and other Israeli officials aboard an El Al jetliner.

There's a photo of me with Begin. We are seated across from each other, his right hand on top of my left hand, in the VIP lounge at Heathrow Airport on the way to or from Washington. Begin signed a print copy of the treaty for me. The photo is on the wall of my home office, the treaty in a closet in the same room.

The treaty, for the first time, sealed Israel's back door, which leads to the Sinai Peninsula. Under its terms, Israel had to evacuate about 8,000 Jewish settlers from the Sinai, which it surrendered in 1982. The pact led to the 1993 Oslo I Accord between Israel and the Palestine Liberation Organization that was signed on the White House lawn by Israeli Prime Minister Yitzhak Rabin and PLO leader Yasser Arafat and the Oslo II Accord that was signed at Taba, Egypt, in 1995.

The accords created the Palestinian Authority for control of the Israeli-occupied West Bank and Gaza Strip and stipulated that negotiations be held between Israel and the Palestinians about the status of Jerusalem, borders, and the return to Israel of Palestinian refugees from the 1948-49 war. Those issues have not been resolved. Israel evacuated the Gaza Strip in 2005, but it soon was taken over from the Palestinian Authority by Hamas, which the United States recognizes as a terrorist organization.

The Egyptian-Israeli peace treaty also set the stage for a similar pact between Israel and Jordan, signed October 26, 1994. Syria and Lebanon, both of which also border Israel, have not signed peace agreements with the Israelis.

BS: *Please also talk about your time with the Baltimore Sun. Were you familiar with any of the folks at the Capital Gazette? I must also say that I am a big fan of The Wire. What are your thoughts on it?*

RG: My hiring as the opinion page editor of the Sun in April 2000 represented a reawakening of my true professional career after more than eight years with the Times, though I didn't get a job on the Baltimore paper directly from the Washington paper. In the interim, I served ten months as an editor for a Washington-based worldwide financial news agency known as Savvis that was part of the Knight-Ridder chain. It went bankrupt shortly after I left.

I did not know anyone at the *Capital Gazette*, which was not owned by the Tribune Co. during my six years and three months at the Sun.

My position as op-ed editor was one of the most challenging, rewarding, and interesting jobs of my journalism career. It certainly was up there with my being UPI foreign editor beginning in 1988 and Tel Aviv bureau manager in the late 1970s. It's been difficult to decide which of the three positions I enjoyed most.

Working at the Sun was comparable to the staff and editorial professionalism I experienced at UPI. It was a thrill to be back in business as a real journalist on a real newspaper, though one that increasingly during my tenure encountered financial difficulties because of the Tribune Co.'s takeover of the Sun and other newspapers ranging from the *Hartford Courant* to the *Los Angeles Times*; Tribune was tearing them all apart.

For me, the continual downsizing of the Sun meant a repeat of the UPI experience—the dismissal of valued employees, both editorial and other staff, the emptying of newsroom desks, the cutbacks in news coverage.

As an example, the Sun had five foreign correspondents on my arrival at the paper in 2000; by 2006, when I offered to take a buyout, there were none. It once had 11 reporters based abroad, a major undertaking for what essentially is a regional newspaper. It's one reason the news industry highly respected the Sun. It was a pleasure for me to be associated with it. And, not incidentally, I made some very good friends there because I often—certainly daily—went downstairs to the newsroom from the editorial department to learn what was going on. Hard news was my first love, and it was difficult to escape that attraction.

As for "The Wire," I believe it was an accurate representation of Baltimore and its crime scene. It was written by two former Sun reporters, David Simon, and Ed Burns.

BS: *And finally, I would like you to reflect on love. You wrote, "The warmth of love surprises by blossoming even in the dull winter of our lives." I love that thought.*

RG: I am no expert on love; I'll leave that to the poets. But, as the old song says, I do believe "Love Is A Many Splendored Thing," perhaps because it can envelop one at any age.

Chapter 13

## Andra Varin—Rolodex Connection: Boston Bureau Reporter

*Wall Street Journal Working Editor, Stolen Leads*

Andra Varin is a Senior Publishing Editor for the print side of the Wall Street Journal. Her career started in Washington DC as a news clerk for the UPI bureau. She talks about covering Michael Dukakis and his run for the presidency in 1988 and when Congressman Barney Frank outed himself as a gay man. She was on the desk at CNN.com the day Princess Diana died. She recalled the day the Boston Globe stole her lead of "Move over Mary Poppins."

BS: *We'll cover the questions and give me yea or nay on any of the topics you feel are appropriate to discuss as a working journalist. Let's cover your years with the UPI. What year did you start??*

AV: It was 1986, it was my first job out of college, I was a paralegal, and it was not for me, and I got a job as a news clerk for Washington, DC. I worked on the features desk. My primary jobs were fetching coffee and answering phones. That's how I started out. Anytime they needed someone to write a story or do something I was, oh, I can do that. And when there was an opening in the Boston Bureau, I think I was in Washington, DC at that time for nine months, I went up to the Boston Bureau and started working there. I worked there for five years before I went back down Washington to work for UPI.

BS: *What was your position when you got to Boston?*

AV: I was a newsperson in the Boston bureau where we worked different shifts. I worked as a reporter and as an editor. There were shifts at night when they needed somebody to sit in what they called 'the slot' and

155

run the editing and, of course, write radio copy for broadcast clients, and regular stories. Every story we wrote had to be done in several different ways. For the newspaper, you had to write two versions of most anything we called a skedded story. We had to write an AM and a PM version for morning and afternoon newspapers.

BS: *What is skedded, a list of stories?*

AV: It's from the sked. There was something called the sked, which was saying, this is what we have coming for you. A regional bureau like Boston would have a sked, and for instance, the headquarters would have a national sked of stories presented. If your story was picked up for the national sked, you definitely had to write two different versions of that story for AM and PM. Mostly, it was tinkering with the top couple of graphs. (Note: sked is a term for schedule.)

BS: *Who did you work with at that time? What names do you recall?*

AV: When I moved to the Boston bureau, Charles Goldsmith was the regional editor. And several people worked for him. Dave Haskell ran the morning slot, a guy named Phil Reed managed the evening slot, and he sadly has passed away. Jerry Berger was at the statehouse. A lot of people passed through there in the day.

BS: *I've got some stories that you did write, and I love your style.*

AV: Many UPI stories, if it's a feature, would have more of my style. The best story I ever wrote when I was in Boston, I was the pool reporter working when Michael Dukakis met with Jesse Jackson. They were discussing whether or not Jackson would get the vice-presidential nod back in 1988. I was just calling in stuff to the desk, and I didn't physically write the story, news wires were famous for the rewrite. I wrote a great story, but Phil Reed really wrote it.

BS: *Phil Reed rewrote it?*

AV: I couldn't write anything back then. We didn't have smartphones; didn't have anything you could write on other than like a reporter's notebook. So, I was taking notes on everything, and whenever I got a phone, again, because we didn't have cell phones, I had to beg local people to let me use their phone, and I would call in notes to the desk and Phil would write the story.

**BS:** *But do you consider that your story?*

**AV:** I reported the story, and I would say it's my story in some ways, but rewrite people are the great unsung heroes of both wire services and traditional newspapers.

**BS:** *Did you get your byline on the story?*

**AV:** Depending on what the story was and how long it was, yes, I would usually get my byline on it. But the byline went to the reporter. There would also be stories that I would write. I remember doing a story that was for a court case, the court was in Essex County, Salem, and the reporter was out there, he called in stuff to me. I wrote it, but it was his byline. That's the way it was done. It's a very, very tight collaboration; people worked as a team. You trusted that whoever was on the desk, that if you called it in, you trusted they could write it up. I also think that deskers, the person who was on the desk as the rewrite person is often able to guide a reporter. You know when you are out at a scene, and something really horrible is going on, you tend to get caught up in things that aren't going to make the big picture, and a rewrite person will be like, okay focus on this. And they've also got another reporter who is out somewhere else, they could say, so-and-so told me this. Can you confirm that with the police chief who is giving the press conference where you are now?

**BS:** *I read some of your UPI stories that came from the People column.*

**AV:** The People column was celebrity gossip items. You can pick up any paper and still see those that have AP now, you have those celebrity news things that were all wire reports, and for the most part, they would be compiled for reports from bureaus. I wrote those items after I left Boston and was in the Washington bureau. The guy who did the People column for decades was named Bill Trott. He had a brother named Bob Trott, who worked for AP. Bill was in DC, and later in the early 90s, I was in DC, and I wrote it for a while. It was something that had to be done every day. My biggest memory of the People column is anything I wrote. I remember we would get clips back from various newspapers. Any bureau from around the world, if they saw something with your byline, they would clip it out, and they would send it to the reporter as a courtesy. I remember any clips that I got from English language papers in the Philippines, no matter how minor the item was on Princess Diana, they would always move that way up to the top. The People column was a blast to write, and sometimes I would do the items, and sometimes the bureau would set them up. Later on, I got a promotion, and the People column went to someone on the west coast.

BS: *Do you recall a January 1988 Wire Service Guild memo titled, "The Body Count," about layoffs at UPI? According to this, there had been 104 employees fired.*

AV: I don't recall that specific memo. I was laid off at one point. I had been laid off from UPI, and I went up to the Boston bureau. It wasn't a permanent assignment. It was supposed to be, but I did get laid off, and I went to work for the Middlesex News in Framingham, Massachusetts. I worked there for about three months, and they had an opening at UPI. Charles Goldsmith called me and said, are you interested? And I said yes, very much.

BS: *You're one of the few women I've spoken with. Were you alone?*

AV: There were plenty of women at UPI. Karen Davies, Catherine (Shahan) Bromberg, Didi Wilson worked there. The Boston bureau chief who was under the New England regional editor, her name was Betsy Ricci. Elizabeth Ricci.

BS: *It is a great job for a man or a woman.*

AV: It was a very interesting job. Now, when I talk to young people who are interested in getting into journalism, I do tell them that it can be very hard on their personal lives. I work nights, for instance. People don't realize when they're young that no matter what kind of journalism you're in if you're doing hard news, somebody has to work a really crappy shift. And that someone is going to be you for a while, and maybe for always. If you're working in television for a show like Good Morning America, there are writers and producers who are in there at 3:30 in the morning, especially now that the news cycle doesn't really stop. I work until 12:30 in the morning every night. Because the Wall Street Journal's final edition closes at 12:20 in the morning, that's just the way it is. I think people don't realize what it can be like. Until you do it, it's hard to understand. For me, it was very hard to work the overnights. We had a shift in the Boston bureau, and you would be on the shift for three months, and that was because it was a guild rule, they had to take you off after three months. Then you would go into the weekend overnights. You came into work at 11:00 pm, and you left at 7:00 in the morning. It was a grueling shift if your body isn't set up for that. I can stay up until 2:00 in the morning but staying up all night was always very hard. You were really busy.

We had clients that would turn off their wire machines because the wires would feed stories all night, depending on what your service package was. Most people who got UPI or AP or both the national operations would be filing stories all night long. In many places, smaller places would turn off their machines. You'd go to the machine and would see printouts of this rolling paper. Many clients would turn off their machines at night, and the overnight person at UPI would be writing. We would send out stories as needed, and we'd be preparing packages of broadcast briefs for clients. We would send those at specific times throughout the night. They were designed to go out at specific hours so that clients would have them for morning drive time.

BS: *And it would store it on the other end?*

AV: No. It didn't store on the other end. Their machine had to be on and running. Clients would turn the machine off when they left, and then they would come in the next morning, and there would be no copy because their machine was off. They would call, literally screaming, this is at five in the morning, and this is when I would always feel most nauseous and tired. They would call screaming; you didn't send any copy. It was the most infuriating thing because they were clients, and you couldn't tell them; you're a bozo go away. You had to resend everything which took time as the morning drive period was heating up. You had other things you had to be doing. You had to go and cater to these people who were so annoying. It happened every single day. I think they were probably told to turn the machine off to save paper. They didn't get it.

BS: *Were you in the Boston Herald building?*

AV: Yes.

BS: *It's gone now, sold, and torn down to build a hotel, residence, and high-end grocery store.*

AV: Back in the day, it wasn't a terrible location, but it was near the combat zone. And now it's funny to think that this is absolutely prime real estate today.

BS: *I have a copy of the Montrose Voice article out of Houston, Texas, that you wrote on July 3, 1987. It's titled, "Voters Stand by Gay Congressmen." Do you remember the story?*

AV: I do remember this story. It was about Barney Frank. Barney Frank had had an affair with a young man who was kind of a prostitute and grifter if I remember correctly. Kind of an unsavory thing. Gerry Studds had a relationship with a Congressional page, which is a different ball of wax. Frank had a consensual relationship. He was an adult. I think he was fixing parking tickets for him. At the time, Frank had not been openly gay, he knew the story was going to break, and he announced that he was gay.

BS: *Yes, he "acknowledged his sexuality" is what I read in your article. So now, it's a month later from the announcement.*

AV: I remember Charles Goldsmith sent me to do a man-on-the-street interview in Fall River, Massachusetts, because he thought that the heavily Portuguese community would be conservative in some ways, and he thought there would be a backlash. He sent me, and I have to tell you that doing a man-on-the-street was a pain back then because people were expecting television. If you didn't have a TV camera, they didn't know what we were. People didn't even understand what UPI was. They knew their local paper, their local broadcaster. I went down there, and it took me a while to find people who would talk to me and understand this wasn't going to get them on TV. There was also some language barrier because some of the people did speak Portuguese, some of the older people. I remember there was a little old lady in black, a Portuguese American widow, and everyone was like, "Barney, we love Barney. He's so good." They felt his involvement with this scandalous young man, that if he was going to be gay, he needed to find "a nice young man." They had a great affection for him, and if they were surprised that he was gay, they got over it very quickly. When I got back to the bureau, I was like, sorry they're not upset at all, and Charles said, okay, write the story; you got to write what you find.

BS: *That's the way I took it. Frank Wing, the Bristol County Republican Committee President, said that Barney Frank's statement "did not reflect the Republican Party." And he said something about they should be in San Francisco and not in Fall River or New Bedford.*

AV: It's so funny how things have changed. I remember at the time sometimes writers and editors would say, so and so would say or he admitted he was gay, or he admitted he was homosexual. We were looking at the language and said no, 'admitted' has a connotation that it's bad. Things have changed so much in the world since then. Acknowledged he is gay or acknowledged he is a homosexual was a big step up from that in the wording. When people first started saying yes, I am gay, that is how many of us in the news business worded it. And then, later on, you would say, so and so, who is openly gay, like you had to make it clear you were not accusing them that they were gay that they had said it. It's just such an interesting look at how both our language reflects things but also how things have changed. There are definitely a lot of things that were different back then.

BS: *Another story I have is when you were with ABC News. It's titled, "Playboy King, Femme Fatale Head Home." Can you talk about that story?*

AV: Yes, it was about King Carol II of Romania and Elena Lupescu. I worked at ABCNews.com, and we did a lot of different things then, but we did write stories that were independent of the network at times. I was always fascinated by royalty, and I knew a fair amount about them. I sort of carved out this niche where I would do royal stories. I was the copy desk chief, but later on, I was one of the two editors that ran the night shift, and after, that I had time to write, and I would write about royals. That happened to be a story about the returning of the bodies to Romania from Portugal. He was not a very good king of Romania. That was a great period in reporting about royals. It was before William and Harry grew up, so there was less to say about the Brits in many ways, but there was a whole generation of heirs of European thrones who were marrying commoners. I did stories on them. Many of them had what I thought were interesting stories, and some of the relationships were very different from what you would expect. Maybe Americans expect a prince is going to marry a commoner, but the crown prince of Norway married a woman who had an illegitimate son. That had never been done before. The heir to the throne of Spain, who is now the king of Spain, married a woman who was divorced, I guess they had it annulled, and that was kind of a big deal. The heir who is now the king of The Netherlands married a woman who is fabulously popular there. She was Argentinian, and her father was a member of the junta that's done horrific things in Argentina. I loved writing those stories, and I loved having pictures. The great thing ABCNews.com allowed me to do was slideshows of royal weddings, royal brides, royal children, and heirs. I just loved all that.

BS: *The web was a perfect medium for that. And, sadly, the king and Elena weren't reburied near one another. She's a half-mile away from him. How about some quick comments about the different places you have worked — random thoughts. You also worked at CNN.*

AV: I worked at CNN Interactive is how they called it back in the early days. I remember sending out headlines on pagers. It was an early version of the push alert you get on your phone.

BS: *I get them all the time. I love that you put them out on pagers.*

AV: We put out the headlines on pagers, and then I moved on to work on the main website. I would say without commenting directly, but each place I worked, my wire service background has been invaluable. Just for doing and working, wearing different hats, turning it around quickly, but being able to say things concisely, whether you're writing a push alert, it's not all that different from writing headlines for pagers for sending out alerts.

I had a former colleague from UPI, who has died now he was in his 80's, but he took to Facebook very easily. I don't believe he was on Twitter. He wasn't the least bit phased by it. What other people were saying, oh, I don't know about this Twitter. And he was saying, "Why, I've written so many alerts over the years for UPI, that 140 characters are quite a lot." I always think about that because there's often a view that older journalists can't learn social media and aren't as good. I think of him because he was like, 'meh.' He was saying I've already done this in a different form. I think this is something that UPI definitely gave me.

BS: *What is your biggest story? Your saddest story?*

AV: My biggest story was the night that Princess Diana died. It was Labor Day, and I was at CNN.com. We had a skeletal crew in, and we had just ordered from this place called Chico and Chang's that was Chinese/Mexican food, and I was getting sick half the night running to the bathroom. The story kept breaking. In the beginning, we knew that Dodi Fayed had been killed, but there were conflicting accounts of what was happening to Diana. At one point, AFP (Agence France-Press) was reporting that she had a broken arm, and I was calling the boss saying, you got to get people in here. He was resistant. At one point, I was just like what if she dies, just saying that to be bitchy, I really didn't think she would.

BS: *Did he comply?*

AV: They did organize a crew to come in earlier that morning to spell us. CNN.com was the website. I remember a flash came in from AFP saying that she was dead, and there was a sort of main CNN control hub. I called them and asked, what are we saying? They were upset because they didn't know. For some reason, a lot of places in the past didn't realize that the dot.com side was there to get the network's message out, that we were part of the network, or that we were real journalists. There was often the thought that the people on the dot.com side of the business were not real. Here we are, and I'm trying to find out what we're reporting. I just wanted to know what the network is saying. Is she dead? Is she not? What do I do? They hung the phone up on me, and they got on this intercom system that went to all the CNN networks like CNN Headline News and CNN International, and they were screaming at me not to report anything.

BS: *Why?*

AV: It was because they were losing their heads, and they didn't really know. I don't have a memory of who that person was, and I'm screaming back, just tell me what the fuck we're doing! They couldn't hear me as they had hung up on me. That was the biggest story I worked on directly. Actually, that's not true; I also was desking on 9/11. I was with ABCNews.com. In the history of the world, that was a bigger story.

BS: *Any happy story or quirky story you want to share?*

AV: There was one story that I've always been very fond of that I wrote when I was at UPI. The lead of it was "Move over, Mary Poppins." We had just gotten a press release, and that's when the press releases were in the mail, from a New England School of Nannies in Central Massachusetts not in Boston, but they were graduating a male. It was their first time. So, I called him up and did an interview with him, and it was a really nice interview. He was a very nice young man, a male nanny, and people didn't talk about nannies then. It was just such a sweet story, and then I came in, and a coworker, John Gregg, was really excited. He said, "Oh my god, the Boston Globe ran your story." The Globe would use UPI stuff for briefs, but it rarely ran a byline story. He was like, look here it is, "Move over, Mary Poppins." We looked at it, and it was the headline. They had stolen my lead for their headline, and they assigned their own person to do the same story.

BS: *Did they steal your headline?*

AV: They stole my lead. Some editor did that; obviously, the reporter doesn't write the headlines. I was so excited, and then I was so devastated. That was one of the most frustrating things about working for a wire service. Often, you would do a really nice story that was very original, and nobody else had and then the local newspaper would think it's a great story and assign their person to do it.

**BS:** *One of the other guys told me that papers would take the wire service names off the article or add a little to the story and take co-writing credit.*

**AV:** That would happen a lot, too. Most times, newspapers would just strip the byline off. Very irritating.

**BS:** *I want to end it now with a picture I have seen of you with a red boa on.*

**AV:** Oh, you've seen me on Facebook.

**BS:** *When I saw that, I thought, 'this is a fun girl.' I want to talk to her. Thank you so very much.*

# Chapter 14

## Tom Foty—Rolodex Connection:
## UPI Radio Network Executive Editor

*CBS Radio News Working Editor, Hungarian Revolution, Peoples Temple Massacre, Tenerife Air Disaster*

Tom Foty works for CBS News as a radio news anchor and correspondent. His life started in Budapest, Hungary, where, as a child, his family home was leveled by Soviet tanks in the Hungarian Revolution in 1956. He spent several days trapped in a bomb shelter. He covered the worst aviation accident in history when two 747 jumbo jets collided on the ground on Tenerife in the Canary Islands. He was at the police station in New York City when David Berkowitz, the murderer, Son of Sam, was dragged in. He covered the People's Temple story of Jim Jones and the cyanide-laced Kool-Aid killing of 918 men, women, and children.

BS: *You were born in Hungary, Budapest. Tell me about being a refugee at just ten years old.*

TF: I lived as a child in Budapest, part of that time; it was Stalinist communism. My parents, for various reasons, were considered unemployable. So, we had our ups and downs, but all in all, it wasn't that bad. I was with my mom when the revolution broke out in Hungary in October of 1956. We lived in the middle of Budapest, which ironically, years later, I was reviewing some UPI stories about its coverage of Hungary that won a Pulitzer Prize by Russell Jones. Anthony Cavendish also covered the invasion. He wrote some stories from that time in a book. Although I was never able to track him down while he was still alive, I'm fairly well convinced Cavendish might well have been an eyewitness to the destruction of my home based on the stories.

BS: *Wow, too bad you weren't able to connect with him.*

TF: In any event, Soviet troops drew back from the capital city of Hungary, Budapest in 1956. For a while, it looked as though they might pull out of the country. On November 4th, by which time the world's attention had been slightly taken away by a simultaneous even bigger crisis in the Middle East, Soviet troops came back in. I lived in a building right next door to one of Budapest's major newspapers where anti-Soviet snipers were aiming at Soviet tanks. The residents of our building were underneath it in a bomb shelter. The Soviets leveled the building.

BS: *You were caught in the bomb shelter for days.*

TF: The building collapsed on top of us. We were down there for several days. The adults were aware of the set up there, and they had some tools, picks, and shovels. Someone knew there was an adjoining bomb shelter on the other side of a wall underground. For several days, they tunneled their way into the adjoining building bomb shelter, which is where we emerged and saw our building completely collapsed. Many years later, on the 50th anniversary, a friend of mine was visiting Budapest. They bought a Hungarian book about the history of all of this. In that book, he found a picture of our building, not totally collapsed, which is a picture that I have. Undoubtedly, that picture was taken when my family and I were underneath the building.

BS: *It must have been pitch black and horrifying.*

TF: Look, I was a kid, and maybe not knowledgeable enough to be scared about it. It was just suddenly a very major change in lifestyle. We had gotten some help before all of this. That area had already been the site of some trouble. We had some friends who brought us some food. We were very well known in Hungary at that time. My mom's closest friend was the world's women's table tennis champion, and her husband was one of the members of the world-famous Hungarian soccer team. They were very close to us, and they brought us food. As it turned out, it was to be the last time we would see them for almost twenty years. In any event, when we emerged, the home was gone, and we were homeless. A friend of my mother took us in for a while, but the Russians had come back. In the meantime, the border to Austria had opened, and my father said we've got to leave. The border was a couple of hundred miles away. They had tried to leave Hungary eight years before when Soviet control first consolidated, and they couldn't make it because I was crying too loud. They had to turn back. I was a baby. We had to stay eight more years and got out in 1956. My mother lost her shoes, walking in the mud. This was early December 5th into the 6th, and she lost her shoes and had to walk barefoot through the woods to make it to the border. There we were put in refugee camps. At some point during our time at the refugee camp, Richard Nixon showed up, the vice president of the United States. That day, I was standing with my father in a line being inoculated. Nixon came and shook hands with all of us.

Fifty-three years later, I was at a book event in Washington, DC. The book was *Enemies of the People,* and it was not Donald Trump talking about the press. It was by Kati Marton, who is a very well-known author. She is the widow of Richard Holbrooke, the famous diplomat, and earlier had been married to Peter Jennings, the newscaster. Before that, she had been the Bonn bureau chief for ABC. She's a few years younger than I am, and when she was a small child in Hungary, her father, Endre, was a correspondent for the Associated Press, and her mother, Ilona, was a correspondent for United Press. Both were jailed as spies, and the children were taken away and left with Communists. The two parents were freed before the revolution in '56. They both reported on it. It may have been the only award ever given to AP and UP jointly because of her parents. They got the George Polk award for their coverage of Hungary in 1957.

They were in rival services. Her mother was the Budapest stringer or resident correspondent in Budapest and helped the two UP foreign correspondents who were sent into Hungary, and one of whom was an American who won the Pulitzer Prize. That was the first Pulitzer Prize that the United Press ever won. So, her mother was involved with that, and her father had an amazing sequence of things. When they left Hungary, her father went from a jailed Budapest Associated Press stringer to their state department correspondent for twenty years. She wrote a book about all of this in 2009 and had a book event here in Washington to which I had been invited. I had given her a picture that's in the book of an AP wire photo I found years before on eBay of her mother, the United Press reporter, and her father when they were arrested, and charged with espionage.

BS: *You found it on eBay.*

TF: I found it on eBay because of my involvement with UPI history. I was searching for United Press related material and happened to come across that. I had an occasion later to meet her husband, and I told him that I have this picture if she wanted it. And it shows up in that book twice. She had this book event in 2009, and I was invited. It was quite an outing, and afterward, there was a bit of a meet and greet among various people. I found myself standing next to an older guy, and we started just chatting, exchanging pleasantries. I asked him what his reason for being there was, and then he asked me the same. I told him that I had not known Kati as a kid, but I really should have given the fact that our parents moved in somewhat similar circles. I really should have met her when we were both children. The first time I ever met her, I was the Washington bureau chief of UPI Audio, and she was on a book tour, and I interviewed her. I told him the same story, ending with meeting Nixon, at which time the guy does a complete double-take, pulls up short, and then says to me, well, you're not going to believe this. He explains to me who he had been, and what this was all about. He had been an official at the US Embassy in the early and mid-fifties. He's a fairly deep figure in her book. He was an American of Hungarian ancestry from Cleveland, and he had been at the embassy. He was a close friend of her parents when they were arrested and was pulled back by the state department in 1956, a few months before the revolution. He was in Washington when the revolution had broken out. He was keeping the Eisenhower administration, the CIA, and anybody else apprised as a Hungarian speaking veteran of that embassy, or legation, as it actually was. Because of the diplomatic crisis involving her parents, he was sent back to be as close to Hungary as he could during the turmoil of the revolution and was sent to Vienna in Austria. While he was there, he got instructions from the state department that President Eisenhower was sending the vice president to the border area for presentations, and whatever, photo ops. His job was to do the advance work and to accompany Nixon to the refugee camp.

BS: *He was in Austria. And all these years later, you're standing next to him in a book line.*

TF: He was there and would have been standing next to Nixon 53 years earlier. Incredible.

BS: *What a small world.*

TF: Three people involved in coverage on the ground in Hungary for United Press in 1956 were Kati's mother, whose professional name was Ilona Marton, the American reporter Russell Jones, who won the Pulitzer Prize in 1957, left UP a little later for CBS, and then ABC, where 25 years later, Kati Marton replaced him as Bonn bureau chief. Talk about a small world

The third guy, named Anthony Cavendish, covered the revolution and was in Hungary. He died several years ago, but his United Press career was a very strange thing indeed. Prior to his being hired by United Press in London around 1953-54, he was a spy for Britain.

He was an MI6 intelligence agent right out of the James Bond mold. He was a professional spy in Eastern Europe, and all over the world, allegedly. He quit and was hired by Roger Tatarian, later editor, and chief of UPI, but at that time, he was the European news editor based in London. After a relatively brief time working on the London desk, Cavendish started getting very high-profile assignments all over Europe. This is a personal suspicion of mine, and I've nothing but my gut instinct and based on his writing, but I am not convinced his spy ties ended when he joined UP. To put him in Budapest in 1956, when the revolution broke out, I believe he was based in Warsaw for UP and was sent to Budapest. His name is on half the byline stories of that period, along with Russell Jones. Since he was not an American, he was not eligible for the Pulitzer.

BS: *Jones won the Pulitzer.*

TF: Jones won the Pulitzer by name, although obviously, it was very much a team effort, and included desk people in Vienna, in London, and New York. This was a really big deal in the history of the United Press because they had never won a Pulitzer before.

Cavendish being a spy and being very knowledgeable, was apparently the guy who arranged the communications that got the stories out of Budapest. Jones was one of the last reporters when the Russians came back in. Ilona Marton and her husband, the AP reporter, were once again wanted as professional spies and took refuge at the American Embassy. Jones stayed on and eventually won the Pulitzer. Cavendish left and went onto other assignments. He was still there when UP became UPI. He stayed on with UPI for several years covering fireman type stories and then resigned and went on to make some money.

BS: *What's a fireman story?*

TF: A fireman reporter is the kind of job I had with UPI. He's the guy who is sent to parachute into some crisis. It was a job I had with UPI Audio many years later. I was based in Washington, but if the story were big enough, I'd be on the plane to South America. For example, I covered the People's Temple suicide story.

BS: *I have one more question about your childhood. You landed in America on Christmas Day 1956. You go from a bomb shelter, in darkness, and possibly starvation to the United States.*

TF: I wouldn't go that far. Not starvation. We had supplies in the bomb shelter. Afterward, we were with some relatives of my mothers who didn't want us there. We wound up with some friends of hers in a different part of the city.

BS: *However, you see the contrast of that dark world and then coming to America.*

TF: It's a world that's very hard to describe. Once we were done with Nixon, we were at that refugee camp for a couple of weeks, and then taken to somewhat more civilized lodgings in a couple of cities in Austria. And, then taken to a US Air Force base in Germany. The exact location of that base I don't know. While we were processed through civilian channels as refugees, I believe Congress passed special legislation to allow some of the Hungarian refugees into the US. I'm glad it was 1956 instead of now, under current circumstances. We were to be allowed in, and we were flown from the American base in Germany. I was a child, and we were on a TWA commercial jetliner as a charter. My mother, who spoke English, was the translator on the airline, and we landed on Christmas Day at a military airbase, probably McGuire, in New Jersey, and then taken to Camp Kilmer in New Jersey for processing. We were there for several days or a week. My father had relatives in New York and eventually reached them. A couple of them came out to see us. We were released to a civilian relief agency and put up at a low rent hotel in downtown Manhattan at a hotel that I believe is still there, not too far from the Empire State Building.

My first true vision of New York is coming up the New Jersey Turnpike aboard a bus and spotting the New York skyline from the New Jersey side. We must have gone in through the Lincoln Tunnel. That's the one that leads into midtown Manhattan. A few days into staying at that hotel, my uncle and a friend drove us around Manhattan and showed us Times Square at night, which was a mind-blower. That was an LSD trip before anybody knew what an LSD trip would have been. We had gone from gray and dark, black, and white Eastern Europe to the glare of neon glitz Times Square in just a couple of weeks. That was a visual experience the likes of which, as a child, is impossible to erase from the memory banks.

BS: *I can imagine it - what a lovely memory.*

TF: To wrap up a little of the business with Cavendish, after I left UPI, I became involved with the UPI ListServ, and a couple of other related sites. I became interested in UPI history, and especially the Hungary Pulitzer Prize. I became aware of Cavendish's existence, and over time, his history as a spy came out in discussions, and I began to try and track him down. Unfortunately, I never did, but in the interim, I became aware of just how prominent a figure he had become after UP. He became a wealthy businessman in England and based on his writings, and he continued to show up at world crisis spots all over the world right into the 1970s and '80s, which is among the reasons why I suspect his spy ties did not end when he joined UP.

In the 1980s, there was some internal political hassle that involved the top leadership of Britain's external top spy agency, MI6. That involved an attempt to smear the reputation of one of the former heads of the agency, to whom Cavendish felt strongly about. He wrote a book attempting to clear this whole history of MI6 and to also serve as his biography. The Margaret Thatcher government of England tried to suppress the book on national security reasons in the 1980s. In the 1990s, he finally got it published. The book is out, and I eventually got a copy of it. It is called *Inside Intelligence*. And it lives up to its title as most of the book concerns his work with MI6. There are several chapters about UPI including Budapest where he went back and got some of his old wire stories, and one of the stories reprinted in the book, he appears to be standing outside and watching the shelling of my home. He was based at a hotel a couple of blocks away, and I tried for years to get hold of him, but given his spooky background, I never could. He finally died several years ago, and I have long suspected that he, at least, continued to be a British intelligence contact, something we'll never know.

BS: *So, you're in New York now.*

TF: I wound up as a kid in New York, and got enrolled in public schools, started to learn English. For the first few months, I didn't speak a word, but eventually, I picked it up. I went to elementary, high school, and college in New York, and wound up with UPI first as a stringer, and then as a staffer with UPI Audio in 1973. I went to CCNY College and the New York Daily News. In 1969-70, those schools were hotbeds of anti-Vietnam protest activity with major stories there. There was a take-over by minority students at my college in 1969, which was a major ongoing local and national story. I was recruited by both the Daily News and the AP to help them cover that. Shortly after that, I got an entry-level job at the all-news radio station in New York, WINS, which is still doing all news. My first news job.

BS: *What about NPR?*

TF: I was a stringer for National Public Radio in 1971, mostly New York, but spent a little bit of time in Washington where Kati Marton was then working for NPR. That was another place we never quite met. I went back to New York and covered a couple of big news stories for the New York UPI Audio desk, one of which was a major hostage situation in Brooklyn, in early 1973, that lasted for several days. It was a national story. I guess it must have impressed somebody because they hired me two weeks later. The office was in the New York Daily News building. Of course, the New York Daily News is in the news today because of the horrible cutbacks. UPI was sort of at its peak in 1973, and I stayed there about four and a half years, and then got moved by Bill Ketter to Washington. I saw him about eleven years ago at a party for Helen Thomas. He went on to have a great career in Boston after the UPI at the Quincy Patriot Ledger.

BS: *Can we get into some of the big stories that you covered?*

TF: I covered some major stories while still being a combination of editor and reporter in New York. In 1976, there was America's Bicentennial, and in New York, the tall ships in the harbor. I covered a lot of crime-related stuff and elections. In 1976, I covered Carter's campaign at the Democratic Convention in New York.

BS: *When was the Son of Sam murders?*

TF: I believe the Son of Sam was in 1971, and I did cover that one. I was at the police headquarters when they dragged him in. He's still alive, still in jail, David Berkowitz. That was one of the big New York stories, as well as the 1971 New York blackout.

BS: *What did you do during the blackout?*

TF: I was off for a couple of days with my parents, in a part of the Bronx called Riverdale, when all of a sudden, everything went dark. I immediately took it upon myself to go to work. I had been in New York twelve years before when we had the big blackout in 1965. In New York, a blackout is rare. Manhattan and the outer Burroughs power lines are buried underground, so it does not get the typical power outages that a lot of other places get. I knew it was a big deal. I dug out my flashlight, and made my way down to police headquarters, in a completely dark city, and then later up to the mayor's home, and covered the developments there. I was there when the mayor called for the hanging of the utility officials.

BS: *Who was mayor?*

TF: Abraham Beame was the mayor. He was an old-line machine politician, a democrat. As it turns out, that blackout had a major effect on UPI. UPI's computers and wires were based in the Daily News building, along with editorial and business headquarters. The wires were silent for about a day. It was a significant hit. Some wires, because of ancient technology, we were able to run manually, but the national, international computer system was powerless for the better part of a day. My operation was run differently. The radio network was down for a couple of hours, and I spent that night at police headquarters and the mayor's, and then went in the next morning. We were up and operating. The New York Daily News managed to get a newspaper out because they were shooting the movie, Superman, in front of the Daily News building. It was the Christopher Reeve movie. The movie company made its lights available to light up the newsroom of the Daily News from the outside. If you take a look at that movie version, you see Chris Reeve and Margot Kidder walking beside the huge globe in the lobby of the 'Daily Planet' building, well that was the huge globe we all walked by at the Daily News many times.

UPI panicked in 1977, Rod Beaton, then president of UPI, really panicked, because of that computer outage. He managed to get Scripps Howard to authorize the money to build a new communication center out of New York City. It took two years, but they established a com center in Dallas, where they moved all of UPI's computer and telecommunication systems.

BS: *Off-site to Dallas, but still operating out of New York.*

TF: Editorial headquarters stayed in New York right through the Scripps ownership, and the change in ownership until 1983, by which time Scripps had sold out, and UPI was under the control of two Tennessee business guys, Doug Ruhe and Bill Geissler who hated New York and did not like the lease in the Daily News building. In 1983, the business headquarters of UPI was moved to Brentwood, Tennessee, and editorial headquarters was moved to Washington.

BS: *They moved out of New York.*

TF: Oh yeah, in my personal opinion, moving out of New York, was one of the major mistakes of which, there were many, in the subsequent twenty years. Leaving New York removed UPI as a major news organization within the same zip code of the people who were paying the bills.

UPI continued in New York under the ownership of Scripps Howard, but they were anxious to get out from under it. They had a money loser. In histories that I have read of UPI, the will of EW Scripps stipulated that the heirs not be able to kill United Press. The bottom line is that they did.

Eventually, the lawyers figured out a way to break it. Most of the third generations of Scripps's, one of whom was Scripps's granddaughter longtime publisher of the Union Leader.

BS: *Nackey Loeb. In 1975, you covered the Eastern Airlines plane crash.*

TF: At that time, the worst commercial airplane crash in New York, although I'm not sure if that is still true. There was a plane on approach to the airport that got hit by wind shear before it hit the runway. It was an enormous crash.

Subsequently, not in person but as an editor on the phone, I did cover what still is the worst commercial airline accident in aviation history, and that was a collision on an island called Tenerife in the Canary Islands, on a Sunday afternoon eastern time. Two 747 jumbo jets collided on the ground, on the runway, in fog. There were reams written about it, as it still today is the worst airline crash in aviation history. I was working alone in New York when that happened, and I sent a message on the UPI system to Madrid to get the phone number for a hospital on that island, and the Madrid bureau chief got me that phone number. I just kept dialing until somebody finally answered, and I had enough high school Spanish to explain to them who I was and what I was doing, namely, could they get a survivor on the phone. And they did. They got me an American named Jim Naik, who was part of a travel group on one of the planes who survived, who then spoke to me for about four minutes on the telephone. I put out the tape, and we put on an advisory about the tape. The phones rang off the hook. Half the radios and television stations who didn't subscribe to UPI were begging for access to that material.

BS: *What a scoop.*

TF: That was from thousands of miles away. That accident had such an enormous toll, and it was a miracle that anybody survived it. A few dozen people did. The guy I talked to had been a Pakistani immigrant to the United States, and he was part of a travel group from Northern California. Some of the members survived because of where they were sitting on the plane. As it turned out, that accident was subsequently blamed on a KLM Royal Dutch Airlines pilot who had been a very high visibility figure for that airline, featured in airline advertising on television and magazines, because he was a pilot right out of central casting. He, eventually, was mostly blamed for the error. There were ground errors made, as well by the tower, but basically two jets at full speed on the same runway.

And in typical UPI fashion, I was working alone. I had nobody to help me chase the story. Then I had to process it to put it out, while the phone is ringing off the hook with people begging to borrow or steal it.

BS: *Did you give it to them?*

TF: That was a very rare occasion in which UPI stood its ground. UPI as a rule, and I wonder if Ketter remembers this as he would have been my top boss when this happened, but the issue did not go to him. It went to my supervisor, Frank Sortino, who was a New York audio bureau manager and program director. Usually, when something like this happens, a major story and UPI got some exclusive like that, we would get calls from people and organizations who subscribed to the wire but not the radio network, and the usual pitch was well we're UPI clients, and if you don't give this to us, we're going to cancel what we do subscribe for. Generally, UPI caved. This time they did not, and I remain very grateful for my former boss, I said to him, "Frank there is no way in the world that I can deal with this working alone and doing my job and dealing with the phones and then spending ten minutes each to feed this material to them. I don't have the time to do this alone, in addition to the mere fact that we have an exclusive here, and people are trying to freeload on it who are not customers." And he said, "Okay, you tell them no." As it turns out, this particular horrible accident was a couple of weeks before a major broadcasting convention at which UPI made a whole big sales pitch out of this coverage. That may have been the biggest feat of my career, and I was 5,000 miles away. It was UPI training. UPI had a fantastic thing about sink or swim. Some years later, covering Ronald Reagan in Santa Barbara, I was chatting for a while with his acting press secretary, Larry Speakes, who it turns out had a cup of coffee with UPI in Memphis, Tennessee, some years before he got into politics and public relations. We were comparing sink or swim notes, and he remembered how he was hired by HL Stevenson, who was later editor and chief of UPI. Speakes was hired as a summer reliever in Memphis, and they gave him a couple of days of training, and left him there alone, and said there you go, you got all the training you were going to get. UPI was like that, because we were so lightly staffed, and it was my experience pretty much everywhere. You had to know your operation both editorially and technically. You have to have a certain level of expertise not only in covering stories and writing but because it was before the age of computers, that involved punching teletypes. In the case of radio people like me, it involved the full path of how to get a signal, how to get a story back from situations where it is very difficult, and how to steal a telephone where you can. Do what you have to do.

BS: *Talk about Jim Jones and the People's Temple that marked the 40th year since the tragedy in 2018. (Note: Jones was a preacher and cult leader who instigated the murder of 918 men, women, and children by poisoning them with Kool-Aid laced with cyanide, and Valium.)*

TF: In Guyana, I covered the People's Temple story with several other wire people from UPI, and I got sent down there in November 1978. We were down there with several UPI wire people, one man in overall charge, Al Webb, whom I had known from New York, who was a legendary UPI war correspondent in Vietnam, who had been wounded trying to help save the life of a soldier, for which he got a Purple Heart as a civilian. One of only a couple of people in American history, but he was the guy leading us in Guyana. We had the Caracas bureau chief, another Caracas staffer, a photographer out of Buenos Aires, and another photographer out of Miami. I had a client reporter with me from a San Francisco radio station because the People's Temple had been based in San Francisco, and most of the nearly thousand victims had been natives of the San Francisco area. In terms of dealing with that story at that time, we were dealing with it in a third world country, with insufficient international telephone lines to get a story like that out. Al Webb had covered stories like that in Vietnam, and hell holes of the world. As soon as we got settled in the capital city of Guyana, we figured out what we were up against in terms of communications. This was an enormous story that was drawing hundreds of reporters. Al Webb and all of the seven or eight of us were sharing two rooms in a hotel, living in it, and working out of them, functioning as a wire bureau, and the telephoto and darkroom transmission center. What Al Webb did was call the New York switchboard, and have the switchboard put him through to the UPI's editor, HL Stevenson, and tell him what our communication system was, and tell him this phone line we were on could not be given up until further notice, however long that meant. Further, the UPI New York switchboard, which was normally staffed Monday through Friday, had to be staffed 24/7 in order for this phone line to be kept open to be switched between transmissions for the wire service, for me for audio, radio material, and for pictures that each of which took seven and a half minutes to transmit. We kept that phone line open for four or five days. The switchboard kept on switching it whenever Al Webb had finished dictating a wire story on the latest suicides. They would tell whoever was on the foreign desk to give the line back to the switchboard to switch it back to photos, photos would have three pictures, and that's a half an hour, then photos would tell the switchboard to switch it to audio, and I would transmit my radio reports, by which time, there would be more wire stories to dictate.

BS: *That was an amazing way to get the story out.*

TF: UPI people had to know how to do this. In general, wire service and this was generally true of the Associated Press, but UPI people had to have a level of self-starter know-how that could not be duplicated in an emergency. It's something you had to be taught while you were in a UPI office, and once when you were out of that world, know how to deal with whatever situation came along. That was the essence of wire service work before the era of cell phones and computers.

BS: *It was sometimes a monumental task to get out a story.*

TF: Sometimes, it involved outrageous behavior. Walter Cronkite, the most trusted man in America, and the anchor of the CBS News spent a large part of his early career with United Press, and he told the story of being taught in Kansas City how to get a telephone line sometimes even without paying for it. How to use a pin to get a telephone connection, and we would all do that. I mean occasionally, one of the things that every wire service person knew in certain circumstances, whoever was competitive, was to get a telephone line. It was usually something that could not be done in telephone booths. But, if you were in an office environment and there were five telephones you could borrow, usually what you would do is take the mouthpiece out of one of them so that nobody else could use it until you came back with the mouthpiece to put it in.

I carried a device in my audio gear that the sole function was to break telephone booths. Not, because of the news media, but because of street vandalism. The telephone companies had telephone booths with glued mouthpieces so that people wouldn't break them and steal them for no particularly good reason. For wire service reporters, so long as they had a phone and they could speak through it, that was sufficient. For radio reporters, that was not good enough to transmit audio material; we had to break open the handset in order to make an electronic connection through the mouthpiece using the wire that connected with them. We called them alligator clips because the end pieces looked like the mouth of an alligator. You couldn't use them in a phone booth because the mouthpieces were glued. For absolute emergency use, my colleagues and I carried a device that somebody started making whose sole function was to break the mouthpieces open and to do the vandalism that the phone company so feared.

BS: *You covered congress, the state department, and the White House. Can you give me a flavor of now versus then?*

TF: In terms of telecommunications, there is no difference. It is far superior today. What it is not is in terms of access and respect for the media, that is far worse.

BS: *The website, DownholdProject.info reads: "A history of United Press International by the people who worked for it." What does 'downhold' mean?*

TF: There have been a number of people who have used that phrase throughout the years. To give you a thumbnail history of UPI related stuff, back in the early 1990s, a fellow who had been with UPI mostly in San Francisco, started a printed newsletter before the internet. It was called 95 (dash) 95, which is telegraphers code for important back in the days of the Morse Code. For the wire services and railroads and various other places, 95 meant something important. There was a newsletter that he printed and mailed out to people who have UPI histories who were known as Downholders. The etymology of that term stems from messages from United Press and then from United Press International managers who would send out about six months, or every year or so, the reversal of the words hold down. The meaning of it is to hold down expenses, meaning not to spend a penny more than you have to, and the word itself is a prime example of how to do that. The telegraph companies, Western Union and the others charged for telegraphs by the word. United Press started contracting two words into one. It couldn't be totally outrageous because Western Union would get on their case. But if they combined two words like hold down into downhold that actually saved a penny. Over decades and thousands and thousands of messages, the use of that word downhold held down the number of pennies spent. So, out of that whole culture, United Press had a downhold history, a downhold culture going back to its very beginnings around World War I. It was a regular occurrence, especially around budget time to get messages from New York saying, all bureaus downhold all expenses. The messages were short and to the point, and the directions were to spend no money that you absolutely didn't have to. Consequently, the United Press people became enamored of the whole downhold culture. Out of that came an informal social grouping of former UPI people and current UPI people going back decades called the Downhold Club.

BS: *Talk about now versus then.*

TF: I started with UPI just as Watergate was heating up. And here we are 45 years later with the likelihood or at least the possibility of a scandal involving Trump that may eclipse that. I've got to be very careful in my wording because I'm still a working newsman. I can't willy-nilly go around expressing opinions about this or that, but certainly, the potential is there. We don't know how it's all going to be played out but have to sit back and watch it. The way it is being reported and the way it is being handled is very, very different. In 1973, the Woodward and Bernstein myth notwithstanding, the Washington Post was not the only media reporting day in and day out. Everybody did. United Press International's Helen Thomas was getting phone calls at two o'clock in the morning from the wife of the Attorney General, Martha Mitchell, with leaks about Watergate. The New York Times, The Los Angeles Times, the television networks of which there were only three were regularly reporting developments about Watergate. Having said Woodward and Bernstein notwithstanding, that is not meant in any way to take away anything from their work or the Washington Post. They did do more and more spectacular and harder work on it, perhaps, than anybody else. But a lot of other people did too.

It was an important time to be at UPI because, in that pre-internet world, effectively, there were two major American internets in the world. That was UPI and AP. Today, on the one hand, you have a lot more sources; on the other hand, you have a lot more sources that are totally useless. They are fake. The agenda of the news world from the 1920s into the 1990s for about a seventy-year period, especially in America, was effectively set by AP and UPI. There were other players in the game, Reuters Worldwide was as important, but not in the United States. In their way, the New York Times helped that agenda, because it was the newspaper that everybody was looking at including UPI and AP. And, when the New York Times broke something, it eventually got on the wires and got distributed to the rest of the world. Eventually, that also became true of the Washington Post, especially during Watergate, and even a little bit before if you saw the movie The Post. That film was a little bit misleading because, again, not to take away anything that the Post did, but that story had its origins as a major supreme court fight with the New York Times involving a particular reporter who just so happens was a former UPI reporter, Neil Sheehan. In any event, in the world of the 1970s, when I got seriously involved as a reporter and editor, the importance of the two major American wire services could not be overestimated. They were the pipeline to the rest of the country to almost all other media. If you combined the entire client list of UPI and AP in the 1970s that pretty much included every radio station, television station, and newspaper in America with very rare exceptions. There are monetary reasons for that. That is not something anybody could duplicate today.

Most radio stations do not cover news anymore. That is a result of deregulation in the 1980s. There was a condition, to hold the broadcast license, a certain percentage of program time had to be devoted to public affairs of which news was considered a major component. Consequently, radio stations, even those that did nothing but top 40 music, 24 hours a day, still had to program a certain amount of time devoted to public affairs. Most of them played a shell game with that to a very large degree, by airing half-hour or hour-long programs related to local events, or sometimes religion at five o'clock Sunday morning, and logging that as a part of their public service commitment. That was not sufficient, and they still had to do an additional amount of time, which was usually done in the form of short newscasts anywhere from one minute to five minutes, anywhere from every hour to different times of the day. And, in order to get that news even if they had a tiny staff of one person, that material had to come from somewhere, and that somewhere was the broadcast stories of AP and UPI.

BS: *How competitive were AP and UPI?*

TF: It was a very competitive atmosphere between AP and UPI. Sometimes, we had to cooperate; that's just how it worked. One knew where cooperation began and ended, and competition began and ended. It was a kind of a strange thing you had to learn in the field, and on the desk, but it was a time when the wire services were incredibly important. UPI had done a spectacular job covering the war in Vietnam, as did AP. There were times we tried to punch each other's nose during the day and go out to dinner at night. That's how the game was.

At the time of Vietnam, and then Watergate, it was the wire services that sent those stories to the world outside of New York City and Washington. In the case of UPI, I worked for its radio network, and for the first year and a half I worked, AP was not in that business. They began a competing service around 1974. UP for all of its downhold cheapness was far more visionary from the 1930s than AP was. United Press got into new media a lot earlier than AP for a variety of reasons, most of them having to do with the ownership structure of AP. The Associated Press was owned by and still is owned by the newspaper industry. From the 1930s on, whenever new media came along, newspaper publishers were generally very opposed to them. As they controlled AP, it was essentially forbidden to supply news to radio as it began growing in the 1930s. United Press was a private company, a for-profit capitalist company, sold its material to anybody who would pay United States currency. United Press went into broadcast copy very early. Ronald Reagan, when he was president, took part in UPI's 75th anniversary celebration. Reagan recalled how as a radio announcer in Des Moines, Iowa, he read United Press broadcast dispatches in the 1930s. At that time, AP ownership forbade serving them, and that pretty much continued for decades and decades. UP got into television almost before there was television news in the early 1950s. UP had a cooperative joint venture, and this is really going to sound shocking, with a different version of Fox. The predecessor of the current Fox News Network, meaning the film studio, 20th Century Fox, where the name comes from. From 1951 on, UP had a joint venture called United Press Movietone. Movietone was the name of Fox Films theater newsreels, which they made and ran before their feature films. With UP running the editorial part of this, and Fox supplying the crews, the cameramen and film editors became a film service for television in the early 1950s. Out of that, as an offshoot, came UPI's radio network trying to figure out a way to make some more money on this. They would strip off the audio of the film shot by Fox and then sell the audio clips to radio stations, which is how UPI first went into the radio business. They then made business arrangements with potential customers under which they could subscribe to a combination of the broadcast wire written specifically for radio and television stations. Stations that would subscribe to both would essentially get cut rates. For the first 15 years, UPI was in that business. It was called UPI Audio. Its name was changed mostly by me in 1983 to UPI Radio Network.

AP had a newspaper culture that ran very deep into the 1970s and was not enthusiastic about media other than newspapers. In the 1970s, that began changing, and when UPI faded through the subsequent decade, AP became stronger and stronger in these fields. Ironically, to some degree in recent years, it's retrenched. Even more ironic, as UPI retrenched under changing ownership in the 1970s and 1980s, UPI got out of the television part even though it had a library of film that, in time, became rather valuable. That television film library now belongs to the AP.

BS: *AP won.*

TF: Associated Press is still very important and is by far the largest newsgathering organization in the world. The second-largest these days would be Reuters, which has undergone drastic changes as well. What has changed in recent years is the technology, market forces, and deregulation that has done away with the needs of a captive audience for news services. Most radio stations don't carry news. If they do, they swipe it off the internet.

The technology of news gathering, and dissemination has become far easier in the last 20 years. Somebody with an I-Phone or an Android in their hand, today has more information processing power, and access to information than probably UPI and AP put together in 1973. Technology that can be used today to gather and distribute is revolutionary. It was science fiction when I was a kid. Someone who is being beaten up by a cop can be filmed and stream it to the world. That is mind-blowing to us that goes back to an earlier age. It's all good. What is not all to the good is the flip side of it, which is the ease with which information can now be distributed, which makes it just as easy to distribute all kinds of malicious disinformation. You've heard about the Russians, and you've heard about a bunch of other people, and you're going to hear more. Twitter and Facebook are not what you would consider sources. They are methods of transmission. They are media. They are not reporters. To end, let me say, UPI paid peanuts, worked us into the ground, and I wouldn't have missed a minute of it.

# Chapter 15

## Ron Cohen—Rolodex Connection: UPI Managing Editor

### *George Carlin's Seven Dirty Words, Fired by UPI for Telling the Truth*

In 1978, George Carlin, the stand-up comedian who was famous for his sarcasm and biting, dark humor, had just won a Supreme Court ruling in a 5-4 decision that said "his seven dirty words" were not obscene. As an editor, Cohen determined that if you were going to report the story of the win, then you have to tell the public what the words are, and he did.

In his book, *Down to the Wire—UPI's Fight for Survival*, Ron Cohen and fellow UPI alum Gregory Gordon report the story of the decline and 'spiraling' death of the news company. The reporting of the details of how poorly the company was being managed got them fired. In 1986, Cohen was the managing editor of UPI. His firing proved so unpopular with the UPI employees, the company just a few weeks later, tried to rehire him.

BS: *How did you get into reporting?*

RC: My high school journalism teacher, the last thing he said to me as I walked out the door was Cohen don't ever go into journalism. You have no aptitude for it. I couldn't disagree with him. I was on the school newspaper, and there were three males on it and twenty-two females. By default, I got to be a sportswriter. I was playing sports at the time and was writing about myself, which was not a good thing. When I got to the University of Illinois, I decided I wanted to join the Daily Illini, which I did right away because it just seemed like a great activity. My father was a frustrated writer and wrote for years and years, and never had anything published, but he was very erudite. I decided I would join the paper. I worked there for a couple of years and loved it. When it became time to declare a major, which you had to do at the end of your sophomore year, I couldn't think of anything else to do, so I put down journalism and spent the junior and senior years on the Illini. I would say that if you weighed the experiences there on the experiences at journalism school, I got a lot more out of it rather than being a theoretical journalist with the department of communications.

I graduated with a journalism degree. It was right around the period when things were heating up in Korea. I found the way to avoid being sent overseas with the army was to volunteer for a six-month stint in the National Guard. When I got out of my active duty, I wrote to the paper in Champagne, Illinois where I hoped someone would have remembered me, and sure enough, I got in touch with the editor who did remember me because his son was a gymnast and I covered the gymnastics team for the Daily Illini. He said, can you get here right away, and I did. It was the beginning of my journalism career.

BS: *When did you join UPI?*

RC: I joined UPI in 1961 and started in Hartford, Connecticut. That put me under the UPI aegis of the New England division, which included the six New England states, and that was run out of Boston. I was thinking about the Rolodex. I never really worked at the Boston bureau, but I worked under the thumb of the Boston bureau for the first five years I was at UPI.

BS: *You go on to Vermont.*

RC: I went to Vermont on a kind of an emergency basis. I got a phone call from the Northeast division manager whose name was Cal Thornton. He called me one day and said Ron, how would you like to go to Montpelier, Vermont. We have an emergency. I had just moved into a new apartment in Hartford, and my wife just started a new teaching job. I thought this is a hell of a note. Do I want to sacrifice my body to a Vermont winter? I called my wife, and she said absolutely. If they think you can do it, then do it. I called Cal Thornton back, and he said to be in Boston tomorrow. Being a great reporter, I neglected to ask him what the emergency was.

I packed a bag and went to Boston. Cal said you need to know how the Boston bureau works. You're going to be in Boston for a week, and we'll show you all the ropes, so when we deal with you in Vermont, you'll understand what we're doing. I'd been working for UPI for two years, and nobody ever got a break for a week. I went to Boston, and I was there for two hours before a man named Al Wade said, come on, Ron, we're headed to Montpelier. I said, what about my week of training? He said in UPI two hours of training equals a week, always has and always will. I found out along the way what the emergency was. Montpelier was a one-person bureau, and the bureau manager and state editor had been at a news conference with the governor of Vermont. Instead of asking questions and listening to what the governor was saying, he said something that was being taped by the local Vermont television station. He said to the governor, "You're a lying son of a bitch," and that was the end of his career. The clients in Vermont immediately were up in arms and said you're not supposed to be a participant in the news. They demanded he be replaced. He was immediately fired. And the Boston bureau said we better replace him, because we couldn't afford to have the Vermont clients angry at us. So, within a space of 48 hours, he said what he did to the governor, he was sent packing, and I was dropped into the strange situation where I was in charge of an entire state that I knew nothing about. That was a very interesting learning experience. All of these things are recounted in some detail in my other book; *Of Course, You Can Have Ice Cream for Breakfast.*

BS: *I've got a copy along with your other book about the demise of UPI, "Down to the Wire."*

RC: I was in Vermont for two years and decided I put off long enough my ambition to go to Columbia Graduate School of Journalism, and get a master's degree. I asked UPI for a year's leave of absence to do this figuring there was no way they were going to let somebody who has been working for the company for four years get away with a year's leave of absence, and was prepared to resign. To my surprise, they said absolutely. I took the year's leave of absence and took Columbia's nine-month master's degree. It was an experience that turned out to be very important to me because the wire service life is very catch-as-catch-can. You hear something happens. You try to find out what it is. You write about, and then you go onto the next thing doing 20 to 30 stories a day, which doesn't sharpen your skills for the more lengthy and analytic material. At Columbia, they made me learn how to write long. The wire services teach you that writing long is a luxury that a wire service can't afford. This rounded out my ability to write long and to write short. I never regretted taking that time off.

When I finished my year's leave of absence, UPI put me in the world headquarters in New York. I was a desk person, and reporter when necessary. I was on the local desk for a few months and then moved to the general desk through which all UPI copy flowed. Things would be sent in from the various bureaus and New York would make decisions on whether things would be sent nationally, and if so, where, what length. That was a big important stop because I was put on the overnight, which is the 10 pm to 6 am night shift, and I was in charge of the report. That was amazing as I'd only been there a few months, and they said, okay, we think you're good enough to handle when no other big whigs were around to second guess you. For the next four years or so, I was in charge of the report for afternoon newspapers around the world. All the editorial decisions were made for the afternoon newspapers during those hours. I either made them myself or had a big hand in making them. That gave me a good background in both writing, reporting, and managing. The managing editor at the time was HL Stevenson.

He was a good guy, and he asked me what I wanted to do with my life. I said I want to go to Washington, not knowing for sure, but guessing almost the entire staff of UPI wanted to work out of Washington because it was the major reporting bureau in the company. He said you know I got a list of 500 people who want to go to Washington, and he asked what makes you think you can handle it. I said, I just do. I think I can show you by my work in New York in the coming years that I'm worthy of that. He said, okay, show me. And I did.

BS: *How long did you stay in New York?*

RC: In 1968, I had been in the New York bureau for only a year, then Stevenson sent me to Miami, Florida, to run the report for PM newspapers on the republican national convention. Here I was tossed into a whole staff of people from the Washington bureau, all of whom I knew only by reputation or bylines who always appeared to me to be the cream of the crop. Someday, I want to work with these guys. Stevenson sent me down to run the report for the Republican National Convention. I said thanks, Steve, I do want to do this, but what you're doing is taking a rookie pitcher, and making him start the seventh game of the World Series. I'm going to be looked at with askance. He said, don't worry, I told the two people who really count down there, Jay Frandsen and Grant Dillman, told them that I've big things in mind for you. Frandsen was the vice president in charge of news at the Washington bureau, and my immediate boss was going to be Grant Dillman.

BS: *I have a copy of an obituary on Dillman that you're quoted in. It reads, "Grant Dillman, former VP of UPI. I guess the thing that stands out most about him was his absolute integrity."*

RC: Well, it was true. Dillman was probably the best straight shooter newsman I ever worked with. I got transferred to Washington in 1972, Grant was the bureau chief, and Stevenson sent me to Washington as a general assignment person. He had told Frandsen and Dillman, back in Miami, that he had in mind that I would be the Washington news editor, which meant that I would be in charge of the daily report of the Washington bureau. A couple of months after I got there, which would be early 1973, and if you know your dates well, was right after the 1972 election, when the bureau and the world were about to be pitched headfirst into Watergate. As Washington news editor, that put me in charge of all of the staff, and they were answering to somebody who was a Washington outsider, and an outsider from New York. As you might guess, there was a lot of clashing of horns between the Washington bureau, which was the premier bureau responsible for reporting most of the news for UPI, and the New York office, which was the headquarters. At times, it looked like we were working for different companies. There were a couple of times I made decisions that were inconsistent with what New York was thinking.

BS: *In regards to the Watergate reporting?*

RC: They left us alone for Watergate. We couldn't do anything more than follow the lead of the Washington Post, because they had that story nailed, and every development as well, because of the reporting sources they had.

They broke virtually every story. We could do the best we could, and we did a really good job of it. We were in the same position, along with every other news organization playing catch up with the Washington Post.

BS: *What were the inconsistencies?*

RC: The incident that most sticks in my mind was the day that the Supreme Court ruled on George Carlin's seven dirty words. The decision came down, and we put out a bulletin that the Supreme Court had cleared Carlin of the argument, that what he said was obscene. I, being an editor and reporter, said, we can't just say that the Supreme Court cleared him. We had to tell them what the seven dirty words were. You wouldn't say a house is on fire, put it in a story, and not say where the house was. The Supreme Court wouldn't have had this case at all if it weren't for the seven dirty words. We had to put the words on the wire.

BS: *It was called for, and it's funny, I remember every one of them to this day.*

RC: This is what I did. We wrote the story, and we put out a separate advisory before the story started, saying that the following story is going to contain language which individual editors might feel is not suitable for either broadcast or print. Then, right before we started the story at the top of it, I put a note saying the language in the third, fourth, and fifth paragraphs might not be suitable. Then, right before the third paragraph started, I put another note on it, saying, editors, the following three paragraphs may be objectionable. At the end of the fifth paragraph, I put another advisory, right in the middle of the story, so nobody could possibly miss it, saying the few paragraphs above some people may find objectionable, and at the bottom of the story, I said to note the content of the third, fourth and fifth paragraphs. After the story cleared, I put another advisory on the wire saying we have just transmitted a story, and you may want to look at the contents of the third, fourth, and fifth paragraphs to see if you find them objectionable. There's nobody who could have put that story in the newspaper by mistake.

The words were pretty dirty and included motherfucker and cocksucker. Motherfucker and cocksucker were placed on a news wire, as far as I know, for the first time. My phone immediately rang from New York, as soon as those words cleared the teletype machine. I picked it up. It was

HL Stevenson, the guy who sent me to Washington. He said, get that off the wire. I said I can't do that, Steve. Those words are the story, and you can't run a story without running those words. I've given everybody the opportunity to take the words out if they find them objectionable. He said, "Get that off the wire." I said Steve; you have control of the wire just like we do. You can get it off the wire yourself, and if you do, you're going to have to explain why you're doing it. I will not be any part of such a decision, and I hung up on him. I waited for the next twenty minutes for the bells to ring with New York putting it out on the wire and replacing the story. The bells never rang.

The next day Steve called me up and said, you were right. You handled it absolutely the best way. Aside from a couple of old cranks who ran local newspapers in the Midwest, nobody complained about how we handled the story. As far as I know, nobody inadvertently put those words in the paper. If they put those words in the paper, they felt the same way as I did about those words.

BS: *So, no blowback on you from New York.*

RC: There was always this sort of dichotomy between New York and Washington. Washington had the most reporters and editors who covered the news daily, and arguably the most important news information that UPI put on the wire every day.

I had an interesting career at UPI in Washington, working under Dillman. I covered Watergate, Nixon's impeachment, and every national election. I went to every national political convention from 1972 to 2000. When Grant Dillman retired, I was named the Washington bureau chief, and shortly thereafter, UPI was sold. I was named managing editor of all of UPI. I was in charge of every word that went on the UPI wires from anywhere in the world. I did that for a couple of years, and I ran afoul of the new owners of UPI because one day I got a telephone call in the middle of the night from the guy who was in charge of the shift in Washington. He said the new owners had come into the office at three o'clock in the morning and ordered him to put a story on the wire. That is absolutely a no-no. I don't care who you are; you don't order a story on the wire. The story was a public relations handout from the two owners saying UPI was going into Chapter 11 bankruptcy, but everything was going to be hunky-dory. The story was to protect UPI from its creditors. I said okay, don't do anything. I'll be in the office in a few minutes. I got there as quickly as I could and killed the story. I locked the door to the office. We were on the eighth floor of a building that they had named for us, the UPI building. The news department was on the eighth floor, and the business end, non-news departments were on the ninth floor. I locked the stairwell doors on the eighth floor, so nobody could come down from the ninth floor and demand that I am fired. I took my phone off the hook, so nobody could call me and tell me I'm fired. I called Greg Gordon, who is the co-author of *Down to the Wire*, and I said get in here right now. We have to write a story about Chapter 11, what it means, and why UPI was in it. He came to the office, and we replaced the story the owners had put out. We killed that story and put out a story explaining what was going on. We did the best we could. We didn't have reporting sources to explain why this was going on. So, we put a primer of what Chapter 11 is. It's not a liquidation of the company. Basically, it was to calm down the clients and the staff around the world. You see the word bankruptcy, and you say my God the company is going under. It might be, but it's a process that starts with the filing of Chapter 11. I then told Greg until further notice, that he and another staffer, D'Vera Cohn would be full time covering whatever was happening on the UPI story.

BS: *You put two staffers on the story about UPI.*

RC: My idea was that if this was going to be UPI's obituary, we weren't going to let the New York Times write it. It was going to be done by us. We were going to tell our clients every day if we had to because they needed to know. They were paying us money. I didn't want them to read about UPI in the New York Times and the Washington Post or Associated Press. We were going to cover this story, and for two years we did. We had a story almost every day on what was happening at UPI. Among those stories, it was not just the process of going through bankruptcy court, but how the hell did these owners get into this way in the first place. It was pretty hairy. We were airing UPI's dirty laundry on the wire for the whole world to see.

BS: *But they allowed you to do that.*

RC: After the first day, the owners didn't have a choice. They could have fired me the first day, and they may have avoided this. But, once the story started to go and was out there, they couldn't fire me. I had a suit of armor on because they couldn't fire me for writing true stories or for ordering true stories to be written. The credibility of the ownership, which was pretty bad at best, was going to be disparate entirely. I didn't think this was going to be a brave decision. We were a news organization, and certainly, what was going on was news. And, if it were going on in another company, we wouldn't shy away from writing about it. Maybe, not so frequently or as in-depth, but I was committed to making sure that every development in the UPI story was on the wire. And, even things that weren't developments, like the investigative stuff we did and found out why we had gotten into such a financial bind. These guys had paid only $1 to buy the company, and in fact, they didn't even pay that. There wasn't even the token dollar paid. The other thing they did was they got $5 million in cash from Scripps-Howard, because Scripps wanted to get UPI off its hands, and they didn't want it to bounce back to them. They gave these guys five million bucks operating money as a kind of like a head start on their new life. These guys took that money and blew it on stupid things - hiring tons of their friends to do no-work jobs. We found out about all this and put it on the wire. We did that every day for two years.

There was one weekend, in particular, that was quite interesting. I told Greg I wanted a full-blown report, a story that would be as long as he needed, and as much space as he wanted. I wanted a roundup of everything that had happened from the day these guys bought the company for $1. I wanted to put it on the wire because we had been putting out bits and pieces of stories for a while, a long time. I wanted something that wrapped it up to that minute. He put together this incredible story, and he handed it in on a Wednesday. I was going to run it Saturday for Sunday papers. I read through it and made the regular editing changes. I didn't have to do a lot. I smoothed it out and helped make it interesting. I wanted it to be perfect. This was by happenstance, also the day that the annual convention of American Newspaper Editors was meeting in Miami Beach. My boss, who was editor-in-chief at the time, his name was Max McCrohon. He had been the editor of the Chicago Tribune and was hired to work magic with UPI. I told him about this story. And I said, Max,

I want you to read this story before you run down to Miami. He said he would. I want to put this story on the wire early Saturday afternoon, as the first story we put out for Sunday papers. He said, okay. I never heard anything more from him. He flew down to Miami, and I called him and left messages saying, you got to read this before we put it on the wire, because this is incendiary stuff, and you're going to have to answer a lot of questions down in Miami once this story hits the wire. I never heard a word back from him. He didn't read it. At one o'clock on Saturday afternoon, I was standing by the slot, and the best editor that UPI ever had, Lucien Carr, had the story on the screen. I said Lucien; we made every effort to get in touch with Max. He's either evading our calls, or he's dead. I said, hit the button. Lucien hit the button and transmitted the story, and I went home.

The Miami Herald printed the story on the front page on Sunday morning. The convention went bananas. Everybody was running up to Max, asking him what was going on, and how could a story like this go on the wire. He basically said, "There are things in this story that I would have handled in a more judicious manner."

This put me high and dry on the clothesline, and I got really pissed off. Instead of him saying, this was put out by United Press International, and I stand by it, he just deflected it, and his responsibility for it. He's the editor-in-chief. He was responsible for it but didn't want to say it. We put another story out on Monday morning with his response. The Washington staff went bat shit. I didn't come in to work on Monday morning. I got my golf clubs and went to the golf course. I took the day off, and I didn't tell anybody. I went out on Monday morning and had the best round of golf I ever had in my life, because I was so pissed I hit the ball miles, way farther than I ever had. After nine holes, I called the bureau and got hold of the switchboard operator, Elsie.

"Elsie, what's going on?"

And Elsie said, "Ron, the world is coming to an end. The staff is about to go out on strike. They are demanding a full staff meeting with Max Mc-Crohon to find out why, to justify why he would not back the reporting of his own staff."

I asked her, "What time is the meeting?"

Elsie said, "Four o'clock."

"I think I can get the back nine in, take a shower, have lunch, and meander in about five minutes to four."

She said she thought that probably would be a good idea. And that's what I did.

At four o'clock, Max came into the newsroom, and in front of the entire staff, he said, "I made a mistake, I handled it poorly, and I stand behind our story." That defused the anger in the newsroom. Of course, Greg Gordon wrote a story about Max apologizing to the staff for not backing UPI's story. That was pretty amazing. It was an important part of my life and reporting career. I never regretted one moment assigning a full-time staffer to do nothing for two years but report on this story.

I would come into the office at about seven o'clock every morning. I noticed one morning that no one was doing anything. The people who were coming on the shift at seven and the people who were coming off shift after having worked through the night weren't doing anything. They were all sitting in the newsroom area, looking at the elevator. They were watching the elevator. When I got off the elevator, they went back to doing what they were doing. The ones who were leaving put on their coats and left. I grabbed one and asked what was that all about? He said, "We know that if we see you come off the elevator that everything was going to be okay." I burst into tears. It was a validation of everything I was doing, and the decisions I was making, which I knew were very controversial. To this day, I've never seen another news organization cover its foibles the way we did. I'm very proud of that. I didn't think it was heroic or anything. I did it because I'm a newsman, and I wanted to make sure that we were covering an important story the best we possibly could as well as how we covered Watergate and the 1972 presidential election as well as we covered anything. I didn't want us to be a party to the bad things that were going on in our company. Silence on them would have made us complicit.

There's a caricature of me that's on my wall where I'm sitting in my office, and on the day I got fired, people wrote things on it. Besides Helen Thomas, Lucien Carr is probably the most famous Unipresser. He even had a movie made of him a couple of years ago. When Lucien Carr was a young man, he was part of the beat generation. He was best friends with Jack Kerouac, Allen Ginsberg, and all those people. He was involved early on. He killed somebody.

BS: *He killed someone?*

RC: He was a very young man, and one of the people who hung around with his gang, one of the men, became enamored of him and made sexual advances on him. Lucien was beautiful. He really was. He wasn't so good looking when he got older, but at that point, he was gorgeous, and you could see why this could happen. The guy who did this was found floating in the Hudson River near the New York banks on the Upper West Side. He had been hit in the head with a large stone. Lucien was put on trial for this, and he beat the rap even though everyone knew he did it. It was justifiable in the minds of the powers that be, and he wound up going to work for the UPI. Everybody else in his group went on to become famous as writers, and he went on to become famous as UPI's quintessential editor. As a matter of fact, he provided the roll of teletype machine paper that Jack Kerouac used to write his book *On the Road.*

BS: *He wrote, "On the Road" on teletype paper?*

RC: Lucien brought home a roll because Kerouac always said he never had any paper. So, Lucien brought home some rolls of yellow teletype paper from the UPI machines, and Kerouac put one of the rolls in the platen of his typewriter, and he typed the entire script of *On the Road,* his most famous book. I heard this story for years, and I said this has got to be apocryphal, no way in the world you could sit down and write a novel or a book on a typewriter with a yellow roll of paper. You stop to eat and drink and do other things. A few years ago, I was driving to Maine, and we were passing Lowell, Massachusetts, where Kerouac was born. I had heard there was an exhibit in the local museum of Kerouac's life. I said I got to stop. Sure enough, one of the exhibits in this museum exhibit was the original roll of yellow teletype paper on which Jack Kerouac wrote *On the Road.* It wasn't an apocryphal story at all.

Lucien was a member of the beats. On my wall, the going-away present of the signed caricature, Lucien wrote, "To Ron Cohen, the bravest man I ever met." That's like getting the Congressional Medal of Honor. To have Lucien Carr, who was a legend, call me the bravest man he ever met, that was something. Lucien's long dead, but he and I got to be good friends.

The other thing that occurred when they fired me was that I was fired on the same day that Max McCrohon resigned. The Washington Post put McCrohon in the second paragraph, and me in the first, which is kind of weird. This was a Friday, and I didn't tell anybody, but I put out a note on the wire to the internal UPI bureau wires. I told them it had been a pleasure working for and with the best journalists I ever ran across in my life that I was proud of all we had accomplished for twenty-five years of red ink. UPI was losing money every year. I was proud of the fact that we didn't have any money, and we were short-staffed, but we never stopped giving everything that we had. We had to spend money, we would go into debt to do it because we were there to cover the news, and by God, we never faltered even through two years of bankruptcy. We covered the news every minute of every day, and we did some of our best work between 1984 and 1986 when the company was in trouble. I said all I have to tell you is never give up the fight, and reach as far as you can even when things are out of your grasp. I put that on the wire. The responses came in from every bureau around the world on the internal message wire. I was there for a while, and I read them as they came in. I thought, my God, what have I unleashed here? They had a party for me across the way called the Blue Mirror. I went over there, and everybody in the Washington bureau showed up, and some from nearby bureaus showed up. A young woman who I had gotten to know from the Bureau in Richmond walked in, and I said, "Carolyn, what are you doing here?" It was a horrible night, pouring rain, and she said she had to come and say goodbye. "You drove over a hundred miles in this pouring rain?" She said, "Well, I didn't drive." She introduced me to a guy she was with, and I later found out this was a blind date. He came to pick her up, and she said we can either reschedule the date or you can drive me to Washington. I'm not going to miss saying goodbye to Ron Cohen. And he said, let's go. He did, and they are married to this day with two wonderful, beautiful children.

The message wire never stopped. It kept going all weekend. There were hundreds and hundreds of goodbye messages to me. The paper from the machine had run out, but before it ran out, it had piled up about four and a half feet high, all tributes. Somebody collected them for me and brought them out to the house. I still have them. It was one continuous roll of farewells and stuff like that. It makes you think, well shit, what I did was pretty good. People had such affection for their boss. I took it to mean, I had done something right, and I was proud of it.

The staff around the world went on a byline strike. They refused to have their names put on any of their stories. For a wire service reporter, that's a pretty big concession. That's about the only recognition you get is your byline. Nobody else knows who the hell you are. Withholding your byline was a big deal. It went on for four or five days. For a few weeks after that, there were stories in the Washington Post and the New York Times about the freak out of the UPI staff over this. On Friday afternoon, I got a call from Ben Bradlee of the Washington Post who had seen the story and wanted me to meet him for lunch on Monday to talk about employment. For the firing of a nonentity, who was not known to the general world, people made a big stink. It went in Editor and Publisher. I was making about $50,000 a year as the managing editor, which gives you an idea of the cheapness of UPI. They hired three people from the Washington Post to replace me. One to be the managing editor for foreign news, one to be the managing editor for national domestic news, and one to be the kind of roving managing editor over the whole thing. It took three guys to replace me. They each were given a no-cut contract of $250,000 a year. To replace my $50,000. They were willing to spend three-quarters of a million dollars a year for three years. I took that to mean; they got a real bargain in me. None of the three lasted the three years. They got so disillusioned by the way the new ownership was handling things, they all left I think probably in the second year of the contract, and they got paid for the rest of the contract.

The powers that be decided to try to stem the constant use of my name in the papers in the aftermath, and they called me in to offer to rehire me. And I said, okay I'll come in to talk to you about it, but this is what I'm going to ask for, a $750,000 a year contract because that's what you're paying my replacements, I want to be the editor-in-chief, and I want to be responsible for every word that's going on the wire, for every hiring and firing, for every staffing of every bureau and this contract is going to be for five years, and it's going to be binding. If, for any reason, I leave, you're going to pay me what's left on it, knowing that this was not going to fly. They never responded to that, but they did send me a letter where they said they were going to give me a dark blue parachute, I wouldn't call it a golden parachute. They said they were going to give me some money in honor of the years of my service. I think it was like $15,000. But I had to sign a contract. I said I'd come in and look at the contract and you have a check ready for $15,000. I went in, and one of the items of the contract was a nondisclosure clause, and I said I couldn't sign this because I'm going to write a book about United Press International. I'm going to disclose whatever I feel needs disclosed, and I'm not going to be bound by the fact that you guys may sue me. I said cross out paragraph #9, and have the new owners sign it, and I will initial it. That left Greg and me with the right to do *Down to the Wire*. A subsequent owner tried to get the publisher not to publish the book. McGraw Hill is the publisher. The owners demanded the right to review the book before publication. We said no. In retaliation, UPI fired Greg Gordon. He wouldn't give them prepublication rights. The book went on to win awards, and it did get quite a good reception. The total sales were not as much as we would have liked because it's of narrow interest to the general public. It did really well among journalists. I'm very proud of the book and the work we did telling the world about what was happening with UPI. It was an interesting career. Working for UPI was the best job I ever had.

# Chapter 16

## David Tirrell-Wysocki—Associated Press

*Witnessed Challenger Explosion with Christa McAuliffe's School Children, Pam Smart Murder Trial*

David Tirrell-Wysocki is a kind, soft-spoken man who covered the Pam Smart murder trial, and was a witness to the Challenger Shuttle explosion, the death of her crew, that included third-grade teacher, Christa McAuliffe, winner of the NASA program Teacher in Space Project. David's story is that of the competitor. Associated Press. AP is still an active news service.

At an Eagle Scout career day, David Tirrell-Wysocki got interested in the work of television and radio. That event eventually led him to work for Associated Press for thirty-three years. From June 1979 to 2009, he worked in the Concord, New Hampshire Bureau of AP. No wonder he says, fake news gives him a stomachache. "No one is allowed to make a mistake." He added, "You hope they would own up to it and correct the error. Now a mistake is part of the conspiracy. It hurts." "In all my career, I don't know anyone who put false information out."

An example of how serious Associated Press took errors was defined by stories transmitted by teletype. A teletype transmitted at 66 words a minute. A 500-word story could take up to eight minutes to transmit. Different priorities were assigned to stories. Urgent breaking stories would go to the top of the transmit list, and others would push down the list. However, if there were an error, the correction would immediately go to the top of the list and sent in urgent priority. Some corrections would arrive before the story got there. "We took it seriously."

The AP Concord bureau was open seven days a week/24 hours a day. UPI was always smaller. "I thought it was a sad day when UPI folded. A whole generation would not know how to write a better, faster story. We competed but were friends. I gave UPI bureau manager, Jim Vandongen, a gift of an AP style book with the inscription, "Please be second, slower and five minutes behind" This was a takeoff on an old slogan, be first, be fast and be five minutes sooner.

"There was an important federal case an attorney had filed motions. I ran to the courthouse. The elevator doors open, and here's the attorney. I asked him to tell me, in English, what he filed, and why he filed it. I called the story in, and then went up and got a copy of the filing. It took a half-hour to read the motion. The UPI reporter came in, and they wanted a copy of the motion to read. I held that motion and reread it, holding onto it for an hour, and then I passed it to her. My story was on the wire already for an hour. It was a competition."On another occasion, Tirrell-Wysocki was covering the Pamela Smart murder trial verdict. "I ran downstairs to a phone booth. One of my colleagues ran upstairs to get the verdict. Nobody gets that phone. I saved the line." One time, he called in a story about a fire from a phone booth that was attached to the building on fire.

In New Hampshire, the one newspaper we looked to for a measure of AP's success was the Nashua Telegraph. Reading the stories in the paper was a test of who made it first or who was better. The Telegraph, at one point, had both news services, UPI, and AP. If you saw your article in the Telegraph, you knew you had won that story. At the time, there were no electronic editions or email. You would wait for a copy of the paper to come in the mail the next day.

"It made me better, sharper, fast, and good. Winning the story proved it. "We certainly weren't doing it for the fortune." It was second nature to compete, though without hostility. Near the end, it wasn't friendly. At the very end, AP bought all of UPI's broadcast contracts. "Imagine giving up all you had worked so hard for and have it been given to the competitor."

"We weren't stars. Many times, our bylines were taken off the stories. We would not get credit individually. Your reward was to see the story. Newspapers would add a paragraph to the original news service story, and then tag it as written by staff and wire reports."

Ed Tobias was a manager for Associated Press in the radio section that was renamed to Broadcast Center. He would tell his reporters to jot down the phone numbers of the payphones at airports. If there were ever a story coming from the airport, they would call the payphones, and someone would pick up, and you'd have an on-site person for the story.

The explosion of the Space Shuttle Challenger was an example of the best good news story in the world that turned into the worst story when, in 1986, it exploded, killing all seven aboard, including New Hampshire teacher, Christa McAuliffe. David was at the launch in the bleachers with kids and teachers from her son's third-grade class. McAuliffe's parents were in the bleachers with them. The weather was freezing. "I was wearing every bit of clothes I had brought." A colleague from Maine complained he'd have to go back to Maine to warm up."

"We didn't know what happened. We thought it was the solid rocket separating." The kids started asking, "Where's the shuttle?" Shawn Wickham, a reporter from the Manchester Union Leader, was there and took a one-wide frame picture of takeoff to the explosion. "It's hanging on the walls of the Union Leader office."

"Everyone was caught raw. I had spoken to the class and given each of the kids a reporter's notebook to take notes that day." People were down. It was hard. Even today, when he sees the word Challenger or shuttle, it gives him pause, and dreams of it. Since then, Dave has done all the anniversary stories of the event watching kids who were there become teachers.

"I covered nine presidential primaries, one of which was when George W. Bush and John McCain were running." McCain came to the office of the Secretary of State, Bill Gardner, to file his papers declaring his candidacy. David's job was to get John McCain to say George Bush's name. Bush hadn't declared. McCain had filed his papers, but still was trailing Bush in the polls.

After signing his papers, Senator McCain sat at the table for the news conference.

"So, Senator," David asked, "What would you say to Governor Bush?"

"Hi. How are you doing?" McCain didn't answer the question.

At three different places in the building, David was waiting for Senator McCain.

"Senator, wouldn't you like George W to be in?"

"Glad to be in New Hampshire." Another non-answer.

The third time, he called out to the Senator, McCain said, "You can ask that question as many times as you want. I'm still not going to answer." Essentially, it was McCain's day in the spotlight, and he wasn't going to yield any time to his opponent. There were no bad feelings. It was a competition.

David remembered the time that Al Franken, who was on Saturday Night Live, did a sketch where he was the roving New Hampshire primary reporter. Franken's take on the plight of the roving reporter, before there were cell phones, was to wear a satellite on top of a helmet and drive around on a snowmobile.

"In the old days, if something happened, you heard it on the radio, saw on television at night, and read about it in the newspapers in the morning." David recently retired as the Executive Director of the Nackey S. Loeb School of Communications, where he had been since 2007.

# Epilogue

## Death of a Press

**"Union Leader Outsourcing Printing, Pressmen To Be Laid Off"**
*by Michael Brindley, April 25, 2013, NH Public Radio*

Thirty-four pressmen at the New Hampshire Union Leader will lose their jobs after the newspaper stops printing its own paper in June.

**"Printing Presses dismantled at The Lima News"**
*by David Trinko, December 7, 2018, LimaOhio.com*

LIMA—Pieces of Lima's history are heading out through a back wall of The Lima News' building on Elida Road, as a Kentucky company dismantles the newspaper's inoperable printing press.

**"Portland Press Herald owner to stop printing Monday edition to 4 of 5 newspapers"**
*by Lori Valigra, January 3, 2020, Bangor Daily News*

Masthead Maine, the largest newspaper publishing company in the state, will stop printing the Monday editions of four of its five daily newspapers starting in March.

*The Union Leader newspaper press before its demolition.*

We learned about the plans to outsource the Union Leader newspaper's printing in April 2013. Like most we read about it in the paper. Rumors had been flying that the company was negotiating with the Teamsters union, who represented the pressmen to prepare for job losses.

At one time in their history, the Teamsters were known as the most corrupt union in the United States. I remembered before the bad years descended upon the newspaper industry, the company was negotiating a new contract for the pressmen. Members from Teamster locals in the Boston area, big, burly, some would say intimidating guys, would come up to our plant in Manchester, N.H. to ensure the pressmen had their issues and pay raises addressed. Today, even the Teamsters are powerless to save newspaper printing jobs.

I loved working for newspapers, talking to the journalists who were working on prominent stories, and getting tips and tales of what was going on in the reporting. The last fourteen years of my 40+ year career was at New Hampshire's largest newspaper. The Union Leader was run by Joe

McQuaid, a publisher who could be as tough as they come at a union negotiation table or as funny as a stand-up comedian at a speech or in his front-page editorials. Newspapering was not run-of-the-mill kind of work.

Newspapers are on the precipice as steep as any rocky cliff on Mount Washington. Subscriptions are down, and sales are declining. More and more layoffs are decimating the workforce. It is hard for the new journalism school graduates to find a job in their chosen career. It certainly doesn't help to have working journalists be accused of purveying fake news.

One by-product of this downsizing of an industry is the loss of presses. These giant machines that would print a new product every day are being dismantled and sold for scrap. The settlers are forming a circle with the wagons. Newspapers will outsource their printing rather than pay union wages to press people and keep up with the tremendous cost of maintaining the high-maintenance machine. Newspaper presses can produce thousands of copies in an hour. The rumbling and shaking of presses as they begin to roll and get up to full speed can shake a building. All that movement means a lot of maintenance is needed.

So, it made perfect sense to sell off the Union Leader press for scrap and outsource the printing. I worked around presses for decades and knew this would be the last press in my career to see up close. After the announcement, I decided to take pictures of the press and, in a small way, document the death as it was dismantled over a month.

The Louis P. Cote Riggers company was hired for the job. John Cote, a third-generation member of the family and current president, spoke to me about what it's like to take down a monster. It took David and five smooth stones to fell Goliath. John Cote would use a hydraulic gantry to move the big pieces and many hand tools, power tools, hand wrenches unscrewing every bolt.

Cote explained, "A hydraulic gantry lifts lower, and travels forward and backward. After we tore apart each section, each print head would lift and roll it ahead, lower it down. We lowered it into the basement, put it on rollers, and moved it to the back doors and into the dumpsters. The gantry lifted and lowered pieces over 200 times."

"A lot of components were left intact; we would lift entire press sections at a time and roll it outside. We coordinated with a recycling company that would roll up dumpsters to the bay doors at the building's back. We used Hardin Metals of Northwood. They crush it down and shear it, cut into smaller pieces, and ship it overseas as scrap metal to a metal refining facility and it comes back as a Kia."

We laugh. We could be sitting one day in a car that has steel from the UL press.

"They'll have these large brokers down in the Boston area, and Rhode Island, New York that buy and sell scrap metal overseas to whichever country is looking for the scrap to create new steel," he said. "We used to go to Pennsylvania to all the steel mills and get the scrap melted down and put into new steel. Most of that business has gone overseas.

The Chinese and Indian governments were buying a lot of scrap steel for years. The Middle East and Dubai were buying a lot of metal. There's more money to ship it overseas. They didn't look at the purity of the steel as much as an American company would. When you're buying steel from Pennsylvania, you generally get a much better product. It's purer steel. If it's coming out of India or China, you're not getting as pure as steel. There will be a lot more alloys involved. It's still a decent product.

John continued, "Scrap prices are really low right now. There's not a lot of companies overseas buying it. Before the Olympics were held in China, the Chinese were buying steel to build all the facilities. We got top dollar for the steel we brought to the recycling yard. It's all based on supply and demand."

I asked John about the economics of taking down a press and selling it for scrap.

"It was profitable to take apart something like the Union Leader press because there was a lot of demand for scrap. In 2013, scrap prices were doing well, so we could return all the scrap money we got and issued as credits to the Union Leader. They saw all the scrap value. I want to say it was pushing $80-$90,000 worth of scrap."

"What do you charge?"

"That was based on equipment and staff-hours. We were probably up around the $140,000 range. The Union Leader recouped a lot of my cost through the scrap."

The demolition of the Union Leader press was a great job to land for the Goffstown, N.H. company. Any salesperson would recognize it as a desirable job to acquire. Cote told me he felt no remorse for taking down the UL press. He knew the paper would continue to publish, just not do their own printing.

"It was dismantling an icon that meant a lot to a lot of people. We were knocking down one of the last dinosaurs. But there's no emotion to me. It was a good job to get. We never like a company that's been around for a long time, go out of business."

I asked John to tell me about Louis P. Cote Riggers. "What are you rigging?"

"We do all types of rigging, large presses, large air conditioning units, computer equipment. If it's something heavy and bulky, we move it. We can lift a lot of weight and have the ability to move it."

"Louis Cote is in its 75th year. I'm a third-generation, and my two boys, who are both in high school, worked for me in the summer. I'm president. Louis was my grandfather. He was originally from Quebec and moved down to Manchester and grew up on the west side. He started in the mills recycling cardboard and was then asked to install small or decent-sized appliances and gas furnaces. One thing led to another. He kept being asked to do more and more jobs. He had the foresight to hire the right people."

I wandered through the pressroom before the doors were forever locked, taking pictures of the press and what had become the scene of the crime. Progress had stolen an old press's future. They were going the way of the rotary dial telephone and the manual typewriter. The pressmen's break room sat empty. Tables and chairs went unused. A steel sink with the sign above it warns, no ink ever in this sink. A May 31, 2013 crossword puzzle goes unfinished. The clock still ticks.

A letter hangs on the bulletin board. It is from Martin A. Callaghan, president of the Boston Newspaper Printing Pressmen's Union No. 3, dated April 26, 2013. It is addressed to Mr. Mathew J. Wenner, Administrator, GCIU—Employer Retirement Fund. RE: Manchester Union Leader Plant Closing.

*Dear Matt: This letter will confirm that the Union Leader of Manchester, New Hampshire, has notified the Union of its intention to cease printing on or about June 2, 2013. All of the employees participating in the GCIU—Employer Retirement Fund will be displaced.*

*I am requesting that updated status letters be sent to each employee.*

*Please feel free to contact us with any questions or concerns you may have. Very truly yours, Martin A. Callaghan*

All employees will be displaced.

Still, I think about the press, and as I go through the pictures of the phases of the demo, only ghosts are left. Ink stained and splattered walls remind me of the makings of a Jackson Pollock painting. Old rubber boots are discarded and never to be worn again. Empty battered chairs kept together with duct tape and wishes await their trip to the dump heap. Blue pressman's uniforms hang on metal hangers on steel racks in a locker room where the lockers have been emptied.

Abandonment and silence have replaced the rumbling. An era is ending. A press is gone.

# Acknowledgments

To Michael, you got this right from the beginning. Thank you for your love, support, and encouragement.

To John Harrigan, thank you for speaking to me, giving great advice, and showing me your hummingbirds.

To all those who answered the phone, returned an email, and trusted me with their journalistic life stories, I would like to thank: Andra Varin, Charlie Fiske, David Tirrell-Wysocki, Don Davis, George Regan, Jim Wieck, John Milne, Joe McQuaid, Judy Koenig, Karen Gray Houston, Richard C. Gross, Ron Cohen, Sherwood Landers, Tom Foty, and Wayne Phaneuf.

To Adolphe Bernotas, Bill Ketter, Dave Haskell, Dan Wolf, Donald Dillaby, Fred Rutberg, George Geers, James Van Dongen, Jimmy Klidaras, John P. Clemons, Thomas Kershaw, and Warren Talbot. There's more to come.

To Kimberly and Don Flodin, you read my work before anyone. Thanks for your professorial guidance.

To Allegra Boverman, you are a fantastic photographer and kind person. Thanks for connecting me with Dan.

To Renee Mallett, thank you for a great cover.

To Kirsty Walker for your skill at interior design work for the book. You are a true professional and I'm lucky you are part of the team.

To John Cote, thank you for helping me with this book's ending.

To my sister, Becky, who never failed to ask how the book was coming, even as it took years.

To the New Hampshire Writers' Project, a hard-working group of smart and compassionate people who help would-be writers become real ones.

To my Toastmasters group, Winning Speakers, you've heard the stories, sometimes more than once. You make me a better speaker.

To booksellers and librarians everywhere. I could not have made it through these long months without you.

And last but never least, to Dan Szczesny, for your editing, expertise, teaching, and gentle way of encouragement. One of my favorite phrases is, "Just as iron sharpens iron, friends sharpen the minds of each other." I knew I had met someone special when you, our teacher, took the writing class out for a 'contemplative walk.' Let the sharpening continue.

# About the Author

Beverly Stoddart is an author, writer, and speaker. She has published her essays in New Hampshire's largest newspaper, the Union Leader as well as the Senior Beacon, and has a monthly column in the Windham Independent. Stoddart worked for newspapers for over 40 years, including at the Boston Herald and the Union Leader. She and her husband own Effective Fitness, a personal training fitness facility in Londonderry, NH. She is a member of the New Hampshire Writers' Project and the Ohio Writers' Association. Stoddart is the Vice President Education for her local chapter of Toastmasters. A prized accomplishment was winning Carl Kassel's voice for her voice mail when she won the National Public Radio game, Wait Wait…Don't Tell Me! She has been married for 44 years to her husband, Michael, and has one son and two rescue dogs. For more information, visit her website, www.BeverlyStoddart.com.

**Beverly Stoddart**
*Author, Writer, Speaker*

✉ BSTODDART9@GMAIL.COM
🌐 WWW.BEVERLYSTODDART.COM